Faith at Work: The Jesus Way

Author: Michael W. Wilson

1 CONTENTS

1   Contents..2

2   Introduction 6

   2.1   Let us start with the good news for our faith at work!..............................6

   2.2   Should we view the corporate world as corrupt? 9

   2.3   "It is not personal, it is strictly business!" 14

3   What does Jesus have to say about our faith at work?...............................18

   3.1   Will you use the name of Jesus at work? 20

4   Is Jesus radical in what He expects from our faith at work?.......................22

   4.1   What is the core of service at work?..22

   4.2   How can we test ourselves concerning out faith at work?....................24

   4.3   The Jesus Manifesto is our core of our faith at work...........................25

   4.4   Do our leaders at work have no shame?..27

   4.5   Are we unique and do we stand out at work?......................................29

5   What is your profession? What do you do for a living? 33

   5.1   How can "what is your profession" be answered the Jesus Way? 35

   5.2   When we follow the Way of Jesus, what about leadership? Is leadership a
profession? 39

6   The Leadership Paradox 41

   6.1   What is the paradox of the Way of Jesus, faith at work and leadership? 41

   6.2   The faith at work paradox according to Jesus 43

   6.3   The story of Joseph as an example of faith at work.............................46

   6.4   Jesus Explains it to us clearly. We are not leaders!.............................48

7   Key Themes – Jesus Manifesto 51

   7.1   Five Focus areas for faith at work. 51

   7.2   How to be fortunate and more than happy in our faith at work (the Beatitudes)
53

   7.3   What are the blessings we will receive from Jesus? Why are we fortunate? ...55

   7.4   Are we known as "poor in spirit" at work. 57

      7.4.1   *Why should our faith at work point to being poor in spirit?*...................59

      7.4.2   What is poverty of spirit at work?...60

      7.4.3   What do corporate leaders know about poverty of spirit? 62

      7.4.4   Is spiritual poverty a judgement on leaders? 63

7.4.5 Do corporate leaders understand that God will be close and hear the prayers of the poor in spirit?...65

7.4.6 Leaders know how not to fall into the temptation to become rich............68

7.4.7 What do leaders worry about at work? 70

7.4.8 Do leaders know what we are working for? 74

7.5 Are we ready to mourn at work?...76

7.6 Will humility at work win the day?..78

7.6.1 *Can we be meek and humble at work?* 80

7.6.2 What does Jesus teach about humility at work?......................................82

7.6.3 What is humility at work?...84

7.6.4 What does the Bible say about our ego at work? 86

7.6.5 Jesus amazing example of humility for us at work...................................89

7.6.6 Why is humility at work important to Jesus?..91

7.7 Are we hungry and thirsty for righteousness at work every day?.....................92

7.8 Will being merciful change the game at work? 94

7.8.1 What is mercy? 96

7.8.2 A leader's role in mercy and kindness. 99

7.9 How does being pure in heart make a difference at our workplace?.............102

7.9.1 So, what did Jesus mean by "pure in heart?" How will affect our faith at work? 104

7.9.2 Who you are at work? 108

7.9.3 When we are pure in heart at work, what is it to see God?....................110

7.9.4 Because of our purity of heart at work, we are going to see God. Who is God? 112

7.9.5 What is it for us to be pure in heart at work? 114

7.9.6 How do the pure in heart at work see God? 116

7.10 Are we known for being peacemakers in the workplace? 118

7.10.1 What is peace, how do we make it real at work and what is the promise of Jesus? 120

7.10.2 How do we pursue peace at work? 121

7.10.3 The importance of pursuing peace at work..123

7.10.4 Reconciliation with Jesus sets up peace at work. 125

7.11 Are we ready to be insulted and persecuted by our colleagues and boss?....128

7.12 We are to be the salt of the workplace. 131

7.13 We are to be the light of the workplace. 133

7.14   How important is the righteousness of our lives at work? 135

7.15   Is anger at work dangerous for us? 137

7.16   Dealing with workplace romances and the real issue of lust for our co-workers. 139

7.17   The benefit of faithfulness in marriage at work 141

7.18   Why should we speak the truth at work? 143

7.19   Why we should go the "second mile" at work? 145

    7.19.1   How should we handle our desires to retaliate at work? 146

7.20   Is love all that matters at work? 148

    7.20.1   Is love optional at work? 150

    7.20.2   Is love a burden at work? 152

7.21   How giving are we at work? 154

7.22   How should we pray at work? 156

7.23   Is fasting important in the workplace? 158

7.24   How do we break the hold money has on us at work? 160

7.25   The cure for anxiety at work is God-confidence not self-confidence. 162

7.26   The danger of hypocrisy at work 164

    7.26.1   What is the origin of hypocrisy at work? 165

    7.26.2   The expression of hypocrisy is through Insincere motives at work. 166

    7.26.3   The hypocrisy of corporate leaders is dangerous. 167

7.27   Are we really treating others at work the way we want to be treated? 169

7.28   Do we choose the narrow way at work? 171

7.29   What kind of fruit are we growing at work? 173

7.30   Happiness and Joy 175

    7.30.1   Happiness at work comes from keeping God's commands and being obedient. 175

    7.30.2   Do God's people find their joy at work in Jesus? 177

    7.30.3   Does God himself give joy to us at work? 178

8   What is our role in making disciples of Jesus at work? 180

    8.1   Why is making disciples at work important? 181

    8.2   How we help co-workers to help others to follow Jesus. 182

    8.3   Why does Jesus want us to make disciples at work? 184

    8.4   What is the cost of discipleship at work? 185

    8.5   Disciples in the workplace are abundantly rewarded in this life 187

8.6	Disciples at work are happy by being united with Jesus in the family of God.		189
8.7	Disciples will be happy at work with eternal life		190
8.8	Disciples have the hope of being like Jesus at work.		192
8.9	Discipleship includes persecution at work		195
8.10	Peace results from discipleship at work		197

9   Why work? 199

9.1   It is said that man has three basic needs in life: love, purpose and significance. 199

9.2   What does the bible say about work? 201

9.3   Is work ordained by God? 204

9.4   Does our work make a difference? 206

9.5   How solid is our foundation at work? 208

10   What Makes a Christian Company? 210

11   What does Jesus have to say? 213

11.1   Main teachings 213

11.2   God and Jesus 213

11.3   Obey Jesus 213

11.4   Love, forgive and judge. 214

11.5   Prayer and fasting 214

11.6   Religion 215

11.7   Persecution and enemies 215

11.8   Money and possessions 216

11.9   Working for god and living by faith 217

11.10   Preaching the teachings of Jesus 217

11.11   Marriage and children 217

11.12   Keeping watch and the last days 217

11.13   Humility and discipline 218

12   Faith at Work Challenges 219

12.1   God's purposes in ordaining work 226

12.1.1   Should people be self-supporting through their work? 226

12.1.2   Should we find self-fulfillment in our work? 227

12.1.3   Are we going to be a burden to others if we do not work? 228

12.1.4   Does our work glorify God? 229

13   What are the consequences of viewing work as God's ordinance? 230

13.1   Work is a moral duty 230

13.2   Can any legitimate work be seen as God's calling?........................232

13.3   Work is seen as a stewardship from God himself...........................234

13.4   Can you be a Christian Business? 236

14   What is the core problem with legalism in our faith at work? 239

15   Summing it up!...242

2 INTRODUCTION

2.1 LET US START WITH THE GOOD NEWS FOR OUR FAITH AT WORK!

We will be doing a deep dive looking how Jesus wants us to live out our faith at work. We start with the good news.

> *I have said these things to you, that in me you may have peace. **In the world you will have tribulation. But take heart; I have overcome the world.**"* [1]

John 16:33

Jesus shows us clearly the way to work out our faith at work. Jesus always has good news for us. We are not to despair. **We must have courage** (take heart).

God gives strength to his people of faith at work. He enables them to be courageous through his gift of faith. God proves himself faithful to his promises and enables his people to trust him in everyday life.

- Can I act bravely under difficulties or in the face of opposition?
- Am i prepared to do dangerous or risky things in obedience to God?
- Do I believe that Jesus will strengthen, guard, and protect me?

---

[1] *The Holy Bible: English Standard Version* (Wheaton, IL: Crossway Bibles, 2016), Jn 16:33.

We live in a world that is full of challenges, struggles and hardships. Sometimes we may feel overwhelmed by the pressures and demands of our work. We may wonder how we can keep our faith strong and our joy intact during such difficulties. But Jesus has given us a promise and a hope that can sustain us through any situation.

- He has told us that He has overcome the world and that we can have peace in Him.
- He invites us to take heart and trust in His power and presence.
- He wants us to live out our faith at work as a testimony of His grace and love.
- He wants us to be His light and salt in a dark and tasteless world. He wants us to be.

We are His ambassadors and agents of change in our workplaces. He wants us to glorify Him with our words, actions, and attitudes. He wants us to follow His example and serve others with humility, compassion, and excellence. He wants us to be faithful stewards of the talents, gifts, and resources He has given us. He wants us to honor Him with our whole lives.

Nathan is willing to stand up to David, the King of Israel. God told him to, and he did. Am I willing to stand up to the powerful? John did the same with Herod. He ended up headless and dead. John was willing to die for God. Consider also Azariah, Moses and Noah. All had amazing courage from Jesus our Master.

- 2 Samuel 12:7–9 — 7 **Nathan then said to David, "You are the man!** Thus says the Master God of Israel, 'It is I who anointed you king over Israel, and it is I who delivered you from the hand of Saul. 8 'I also gave you your master's house and your master's wives into your care, and I gave you the house of Israel and Judah; and if that had been too little, I would have added to you many more things like these! 9 **'Why have you despised the word of the Master by doing evil in His sight?** You have struck down Uriah the Hittite with the sword, have taken his wife to be your wife, and have killed him with the sword of the sons of Ammon.

- 2 Chronicles 26:16–18 — 16 But when he became strong, **his heart was so proud that he acted corruptly, and he was unfaithful to the Master his God**, for he entered the temple of the Master to burn incense on the altar of incense. 17 Then Azariah the priest entered after him and with him eighty priests of the Master, valiant men. 18 **They opposed Uzziah the king and said to him**, "It is not for you, Uzziah, to burn incense to the Master, but for the priests, the sons of Aaron who are consecrated to burn incense. Get out of the sanctuary, for you have been unfaithful and will have no honor from the Master God."

- Mark 6:18 — 18 For **John had been saying to Herod, "It is not lawful for you to have your brother's wife."**

- Hebrews 11:7 — 7 By faith Noah, **being warned by God about things not yet seen**, in reverence prepared an ark for the salvation of his household, by which he condemned the world, and became an heir of the righteousness which is according to faith.

- Hebrews 11:24–27 — 24 By faith Moses, when he had grown up, refused to be called the son of Pharaoh's daughter, 25 **choosing rather to endure ill-treatment with the people of God than to enjoy the passing pleasures of sin**, 26 considering the reproach of the Messiah greater riches than the treasures of Egypt; for he was looking to the reward. 27 **By faith he left Egypt, not fearing the wrath of the king; for he endured, as seeing Him who is unseen**.

Online version: Let us start with the good news for our faith at work! | Jesus Quotes and God Thoughts (wordpress.com)

YouTube: https://youtu.be/wHxGda-QCKc

2.2 Should we view the corporate world as corrupt?

We will explore the tools Jesus gives us to work out our faith at work. As a backdrop, it will help to understand the nature of the workplace.

This is where some basic theology comes into play. This is the biblical view of reality. Corporations are made up of people. What are the implications of that?

How does Jesus see things? There is only one who is good and that is God (and His Son).

> *Why do you ask me about what is good?* ***There is only one who is good.***[2]

Matthew 19:17

Jesus knows evil is real and that we are evil. The followers of Jesus have good news at work. God will deliver us from evil. We must be aware, however, that we live and work in an evil world.

> *And lead us not into temptation but* ***deliver us from evil***. [3]

Matthew 6:13

Jesus knows what our corporate leaders are thinking in their hearts. That is a reality check.

> *But Jesus, knowing their thoughts, said,* ***"Why do you think evil in your hearts?"***[4]

Matthew 9:4

---

[2] *The Holy Bible: English Standard Version* (Wheaton, IL: Crossway Bibles, 2016), Mt 19:17.

[3] *The Holy Bible: English Standard Version* (Wheaton, IL: Crossway Bibles, 2016), Mt 6:13.

[4] *The Holy Bible: English Standard Version* (Wheaton, IL: Crossway Bibles, 2016), Mt 9:4.

We may hear good things coming out of the mouth of our leaders and our colleagues. Should we be concerned? Jesus has some answers for that.

[34] You brood of vipers! ***How can you speak good when you are*** ***evil?*** *For out of the abundance of the heart the mouth speaks.* [5]

Matthew 12:34-37

And this is the judgment: the light has come into the world, and ***people loved the darkness rather than the light because their*** ***works were evil.***[6]

The Apostle Paul clearly sees this.

For there is no distinction: ***for all have sinned and fall short of the*** ***glory of God,***[7]

Romans 3:23

What then? Are we Jews any better off? No, not at all. ***For we have*** ***already charged that all,*** *[both Jews and Greeks],* ***are under sin***, *[10] as it is written:*

"None is righteous, no, not one; no one understands; no one ***seeks for God***. *All have turned aside; together they have become worthless;* ***no one does good, not even one.***" *"Their throat is an open grave; they use their tongues to deceive." "The venom of asps is under their lips." "Their mouth is full of curses and bitterness." "Their feet are swift to shed blood; in their paths are ruin and misery,*

---

[5] *The Holy Bible: English Standard Version* (Wheaton, IL: Crossway Bibles, 2016), Mt 12:34–37.

[6] *The Holy Bible: English Standard Version* (Wheaton, IL: Crossway Bibles, 2016), Jn 3:19.

[7] *The Holy Bible: English Standard Version* (Wheaton, IL: Crossway Bibles, 2016), Ro 3:22–23.

and the way of peace they have not known." "There is no fear of God
before their eyes." [8]

Romans 3:9-18

In case it is not clear, here is more:

- But he answered them, "**An evil and adulterous generation seeks for a sign**, but no sign will be given to it except the sign of the prophet Jonah.[9]
- Look carefully then how you walk, not as unwise but as wise, [16] making the best use of the time, because **the days are evil**.[10]
- For we do not wrestle against flesh and blood, but against the rulers, against the authorities, against the cosmic powers over this present darkness, **against the spiritual forces of evil in the heavenly places**.[11]
- Therefore, take up the whole armor of God, **that you may be able to withstand in the evil day**, and having done all, to stand firm. [12]
- **Take care, brothers, lest there be in any of you an evil, unbelieving heart,** leading you to fall away from the living God. [13]
- We know that we are from God, and **the universe lies in the power of the evil one.** [14]

The theology at play here is the doctrine of total depravity.

The doctrine of total depravity is an acknowledgement that the Bible teaches that as a result of the fall of man (Genesis 3:6)

---

[8] *The Holy Bible: English Standard Version* (Wheaton, IL: Crossway Bibles, 2016), Ro 3:9–18.

[9] *The Holy Bible: English Standard Version* (Wheaton, IL: Crossway Bibles, 2016), Mt 12:39.

[10] *The Holy Bible: English Standard Version* (Wheaton, IL: Crossway Bibles, 2016), Eph 5:15–16.

[11] *The Holy Bible: English Standard Version* (Wheaton, IL: Crossway Bibles, 2016), Eph 6:12.

[12] *The Holy Bible: English Standard Version* (Wheaton, IL: Crossway Bibles, 2016), Eph 6:13.

[13] *The Holy Bible: English Standard Version* (Wheaton, IL: Crossway Bibles, 2016), Heb 3:12.

[14] *The Holy Bible: English Standard Version* (Wheaton, IL: Crossway Bibles, 2016), 1 Jn 5:19.

every part of man—his mind, will, emotions and flesh—have been corrupted by sin. In other words, sin affects all areas of our being including who we are and what we do. It penetrates to the very core of our being so that everything is tainted by sin and "…all our righteous acts are like filthy rags" before a holy God (Isaiah 64:6). It acknowledges that the Bible teaches that we sin because we are sinners by nature. Or, as Jesus says, "So every good tree bears good fruit, but the bad tree bears bad fruit. A good tree cannot produce bad fruit, nor can a bad tree produce good fruit." (Matthew 7:17-18).

The total depravity of man is seen throughout the Bible. *Man's heart is "deceitful and desperately wicked" (Jeremiah 17:9). The Bible also teaches us that man is born dead in transgression and sin (Psalm 51:5, Psalm 58:3, Ephesians 2:1-5). The Bible teaches that because unregenerate man is "dead in transgressions" (Ephesians 2:5), he is held captive by a love for sin (John 3:19; John 8:34) so that he will not seek God (Romans 3:10-11) because he loves the darkness (John 3:19) and does not understand the things of God (1 Corinthians 2:14). Therefore, men suppress the truth of God in unrighteousness (Romans 1:18) and continue to willfully live in sin. Because they are totally depraved, this sinful lifestyle seems right to men (Proverbs 14:12) so they reject the gospel of Christ as foolishness (1 Corinthians 1:18) and their mind is "hostile toward God; for it does not subject itself to the law of God, for it is unable to do so" (Romans 8:7).*

The Apostle Paul summarizes the total depravity of man *in Romans 3:9-18. He begins this passage by saying that "both Jews and Greeks are all under sin." Simply put, this means that man is under the control of sin or is controlled by his sin nature (his natural tendency to sin). The fact that unregenerate people are controlled by their selfish, sinful tendencies should not come as a surprise to any parent. What parent must teach his or her child to be selfish, to covet what someone else has or to lie? Those actions come naturally from the child's sin nature. Instead, the parent must devote much time to teaching the child the importance of telling the truth, of sharing instead of being selfish, of obeying instead of rebelling, etc.*

Then in the rest of this passage Paul quotes extensively from the Old Testament in explaining how sinful man really is. *For example, we see that 1—no one is without sin, 2—no one seeks after God, 3—there is no one who is good, 4—their speech is corrupted by sin, 5—their actions are corrupted by sin, and 6—above all, they have no fear of God. So, when one considers even these few verses, it becomes abundantly clear the Bible does indeed teach that fallen*

> man is "totally depraved," because sin affects all of him including his mind, will and emotions so that "there is none who does good, no not one" (Romans 3:12).

Source: Total depravity - is it biblical? | GotQuestions.org

The corporate workplace, its leaders, and employees, are made up of collective groups who are depraved and evil. Jesus sees this clearly.

> **If you then, who are evil,** know how to give good gifts to your children, how much more will your Father who is in heaven give good things to those who ask him! [15]

Online version: Should we view the corporate world as corrupt? | Jesus Quotes and God Thoughts (wordpress.com)

YouTube: https://youtu.be/4FQTFpTk6Z8

---

[15] *The Holy Bible: English Standard Version* (Wheaton, IL: Crossway Bibles, 2016), Mt 7:11.

2.3 "IT IS NOT PERSONAL, IT IS STRICTLY BUSINESS!"

"It is not personal; it is strictly business!"

Michael Corleone (The Godfather movie)

https://youtu.be/JyxzZtKNVUc

This is the underbelly of the corporate world that clearly needs to be understood. I have heard it before in the corporate leaders. Sometimes it has been said aloud and clearly. Many times, it is certainly the underlying guiding principle. It is a mistake to believe that corporations are looking out for the best interests of people of faith or employees in general. Most of the time they are not.

This is not to say that we do not have any Christian leaders or Christian businesses. Most publicly traded companies are led this way. We should be aware of that and pray accordingly.

We live in a corporate environment that can be organized against people of faith. Many days we are fighting evil. This is real.

- *If you were of the world, the world would love you as its own; **but because you are not of the world, but I chose you out of the world, therefore the world hates you**.* [2016]

- **Do not be conformed to this world**, but be transformed by the renewal of your mind, that by testing you may discern what is the will of God, what is good, acceptable, and perfect. [17]

- Where is the one who is wise? Where is the scribe? Where is the debater of this age? **Has not God made foolish the wisdom of the world**? [18]

- **Now we have received not the spirit of the world,** but the Spirit who is from God, that we might understand the things freely given us by God. [19]

- In their case **the god of this world has blinded the minds** of the unbelievers, to keep them from understanding something clearly at last of the gospel of the glory of the Messiah, who is the image of God. [520]

- In the same way we also, when we were children, were enslaved to the elementary principles of the world [21]

- And you were dead in the trespasses and sins [2] in which you once walked, following the course of this world, following the prince of the power of the air, the spirit that is now at work in the sons of disobedience— [3] among whom we all once lived in the passions of our flesh, carrying out the desires of the body and the mind, and were by nature children of wrath, like the rest of mankind. [22]

- For the grace of God has appeared, bringing salvation for all people, [12] **training us to renounce ungodliness and worldly passions,** and to live self-controlled, upright, and godly lives in the present age, [13] waiting for our blessed hope, the appearing of the glory of our great God and Savior Jesus Christ, [14] **who gave**

---

[16] *The Holy Bible: English Standard Version* (Wheaton, IL: Crossway Bibles, 2016), Jn 15:19–20.

[17] *The Holy Bible: English Standard Version* (Wheaton, IL: Crossway Bibles, 2016), Ro 12:2.

[18] *The Holy Bible: English Standard Version* (Wheaton, IL: Crossway Bibles, 2016), 1 Co 1:20.

[19] *The Holy Bible: English Standard Version* (Wheaton, IL: Crossway Bibles, 2016), 1 Co 2:12.

[20] *The Holy Bible: English Standard Version* (Wheaton, IL: Crossway Bibles, 2016), 2 Co 4:4–5.

[21] *The Holy Bible: English Standard Version* (Wheaton, IL: Crossway Bibles, 2016), Ga 4:3.

[22] *The Holy Bible: English Standard Version* (Wheaton, IL: Crossway Bibles, 2016), Eph 2:1–3.

himself for us to redeem us from all lawlessness and to purify for himself a people for his own possession who are zealous for good works. [23]

- Religion that is pure and undefiled before God the Father is this: to visit orphans and widows in their affliction, **and to keep oneself unstained from the world**. [24]
- You adulterous people! **Do you not know that friendship with the world is enmity with God?** Therefore, whoever wishes to be a friend of the world makes himself an enemy of God.[25]
- **Do not love the world or the things in the world.** If anyone **loves the world, the love of the Father is not in him.** [16] **For all that is in the world—the desires of the flesh and the desires of the eyes and pride of life—is not from the Father but is from the world**. [17] And the world is passing away along with its desires, but whoever does the will of God abides forever. [26]
- **Do not be surprised, brothers, that the world hates you**. [14] We know that we have passed out of death into life, because we love the brothers. Whoever does not love abides in death. [15] Everyone who hates his brother is a murderer, and you know that no murderer has eternal life abiding in him. [27]
- We know that we are from God, and **the entire world lies in the power of the evil one.** [28]
- And the great dragon was thrown down, that ancient serpent, who is called the devil and Satan, **the deceiver of the entire world**—he was thrown down to the earth, and his angels were thrown down with him.[29]

Online Version: It is not personal; it is strictly business! | Jesus Quotes and God Thoughts (wordpress.com)

---

[23] *The Holy Bible: English Standard Version* (Wheaton, IL: Crossway Bibles, 2016), Tt 2:11–14.

[24] *The Holy Bible: English Standard Version* (Wheaton, IL: Crossway Bibles, 2016), Jas 1:27.

[25] *The Holy Bible: English Standard Version* (Wheaton, IL: Crossway Bibles, 2016), Jas 4:4.

[26] *The Holy Bible: English Standard Version* (Wheaton, IL: Crossway Bibles, 2016), 1 Jn 2:15–17.

[27] *The Holy Bible: English Standard Version* (Wheaton, IL: Crossway Bibles, 2016), 1 Jn 3:13–15.

[28] *The Holy Bible: English Standard Version* (Wheaton, IL: Crossway Bibles, 2016), 1 Jn 5:19.

[29] *The Holy Bible: English Standard Version* (Wheaton, IL: Crossway Bibles, 2016), Re 12:9.

YouTube: https://youtu.be/_gbjTwxIlBw

3 WHAT DOES JESUS HAVE TO SAY ABOUT OUR FAITH AT WORK?

Jesus has a plan for us at work: The power of the Holy Spirit, working in us and our Christian colleagues, is ready to transform our workplace and the corporations we work for. To transform the workplace, Jesus needs to transform how we act out our faith at work. It will be an exciting journey. Let us decide to start. Jesus is ready. Are we?

Jesus has a lot to say about our faith at work. It is not what I thought he would say. I have stepped back because what Jesus advocates is antithetical to normal work models and clearly counter to the "servant leader" model.

- God places us in a position of prominence because we have a servant's heart and always place ourselves last.
- Our goal is not to lead. Never, ever, ever.
- Our goal is not to be first. Not today and not in the future.
- Our Goal is always to serve and love. That is, it and that is enough.

What Jesus has to say will shock what you have learned in business school and church.

- Imagine you are in your MBA class and the professor tells you must be poor in spirit or pure in heart. It is not going to happen. No way!
- Where is the MBA course on love? Yet, as colleagues, love is the job that Jesus gives us to do every day.
- Where is the MBA course on always being last? It does not exist.
- Work, the world's way, is about getting ahead and getting promoted. It is about personal influence, recognition, and promotion.
- Are we ready to show gentleness, love, joy, kindness, mercy, patience and more about the way of Jesus at work?

I had a CEO once tell me that during my next presentation I need to quit talking about what others had done and talk about what I had done. And she was serious. I am ashamed to admit I took her advice. She would have been angry if I had not. I have always regretted doing that. Not a highlight of my walk with Jesus.

Jesus is clear. "**Many who are first will be last, and the last first.**"

Is Jesus serious? Yes, He is. He means it. Are you ready for this?

- You might get fired for talking about the Way of Jesus or using the name of Jesus.

- Matthew 16:24 — Then Jesus said to His disciples, **"If anyone wishes to come after Me, he must deny himself, and take up his cross and follow Me."**
- Acts 21:13 — Then Paul answered, "What are you doing, weeping, and breaking my heart? For I am ready not only to be bound, **but even to die at Jerusalem for the name of the Master Jesus.**"
- Philippians 3:7 — But whatever things were gain to me, **those things I have counted as loss for the sake of the Messiah**.
- 1 Peter 2:11 — Beloved, I urge you as aliens and strangers to **abstain from fleshly lusts which wage war against the soul**.
- Matthew 5:29 — "If your right eye makes you stumble, tear it out and throw it from you; for **it is better for you to lose one of the parts of your body, than for your whole body to be thrown into hell**.

Good news: We have good news. Jesus gives us the power of the Holy Spirit to deny ourselves at work and focus on serving others. We are freed from the slavery of are we going to get that next promotion.

Online Version: Is Jesus radical in what He expects from our faith at work? What is the core of service? | Digital Business (wordpress.com)

4.2 How can we test ourselves concerning out faith at work?

Good news: At work, we get used to performance reviews, 360 surveys, feedback sessions (formal and informal) and surveys where we are tested in terms of our competence. Some of it is helpful. Much of it is not. For people of faith, there is a better way. It is the way of Jesus. The Holy Spirit will enlighten us.

> ***Test yourselves to see if you are in the faith [at work]****; examine yourselves! Or do you not recognize this about yourselves, that Jesus the Messiah is in you — **unless indeed you fail the test**?*

2 Corinthians 13:5

How does our faith at work look like when we assess ourselves with this as the standard?

What might we consider our charge to be as we work out our faith at work? How are we doing with our co-workers? How are we doing with our supervisor? What did our peacemaking look like today? How merciful were we? How humble did we act?

- Fortunate [blessed] are the **poor in spirit**, for the kingdom of heaven is theirs.
- Fortunate are those who **mourn**, for they will be comforted.
- Fortunate are the **humble**, for they will inherit the earth.
- Fortunate are those who **hunger and thirst for righteousness**, for they will be filled.
- Fortunate are the **merciful**, for they will be shown mercy.
- Fortunate are the **pure in heart**, for they will see God.
- Fortunate are the **peacemakers**, for they will be called sons of God.
- Fortunate are those who are **persecuted because of righteousness**, for the kingdom of heaven is theirs."

The "Jesus Way" goal for our faith at work: We need to test ourselves to see if we are following the way of Jesus at work. He has given us the standards. Others will not do this for you. Your supervisor will not give you an evaluation on how well you love your colleagues. You will not earn a raise because you are more merciful than your co-workers.

Online Version: How can we test ourselves concerning out faith at work? | Digital Business (wordpress.com)

4.3 THE JESUS MANIFESTO IS OUR CORE OF OUR FAITH AT WORK.

The Jesus Manifesto (aka Sermon on the Mount: Matthew 5 - 7) is the best-known part of the teaching of Jesus, though arguably it is the least understood, and certainly it is the least obeyed. It is the nearest thing to a manifesto that he ever uttered, for it is his own description of what he wanted his followers to be and to do. It is the core teaching of how to live our faith out at work. We must spend time understanding the goal Jesus has in mind for us at work and home. We find it in the manifesto.

The years which followed the end of the second world war in 1945 were marked by innocent idealism. My dad was a part of this generation. The ghastly nightmare was over. 'Reconstruction' was the universal goal.

- Six years of destruction and devastation belonged to the past; the task now was to build a new world of co-operation and peace.
- But idealism's twin sister is disillusion—disillusion with those who do not share the ideal or (worse) who oppose it or (worse still) who betray it.
- And disillusion with what *is* keeps feeding the idealism of what *could be*.

We seem to have been passing through decades of disillusion. Each rising generation is disaffected with the world it has inherited. Sometimes the reaction has been naive, though that is not to say it has been insincere. The horrors of Vietnam were not ended by those who gave out flowers and chalked up their slogan 'Make love not war,' yet their protest did not pass unnoticed.

The "Jesus Way" goal for our faith at work: We are to follow the Way of Jesus at work. We need to focus on all of it, not just part. A holistic approach is critical. That is our goal. Anything else will bring down the wrath of Jesus on our hypocrisy.

Others today are repudiating, by adopting socialism and Marxism to counteract the greedy affluence of the west which grows ever fatter. It happens either by the spoliation of the natural environment or by the exploitation of developing nations or by both at once; and they register the completeness of their rejection by living simply, dressing casually, going barefoot, and avoiding waste. Instead of the shames of bourgeois socializing they hunger for authentic relationships of love.

It is happening at work. We will not be able to avoid it at all as we witness about the good news of Jesus. Our co-workers will notice.

They despise the superficiality of both irreligious materialism and religious conformism, for they sense that there is an awesome 'reality' far bigger than these trivialities, and they seek this elusive 'transcendental' dimension through meditation, drugs, or sex.

- They abominate the very concept of the rat race and consider it more honorable to drop out than to take part.
- All this is symptomatic of the inability of the younger generation to accommodate themselves to the status quo or acclimatize themselves to the prevailing culture.

The "Jesus Way" goal for our faith at work: Jesus laid it out for us in His Manifesto. Jesus wants us to take it seriously. He really does want us to be merciful, humble, pure in heart, etc. He is clear. We need to take it seriously.

Online Version: Are we unique and do we stand out at work? | Digital Business (wordpress.com)

5 WHAT IS YOUR PROFESSION? WHAT DO YOU DO FOR A LIVING?

What does Jesus think our profession is? What does Jesus think our purpose at work is? Jesus has a lot to say about our purpose at work. Do we know it? Do we live it?

- How about we spend our day loving our colleagues?
- How much time would that take?
- Should we focus on serving others and place ourselves as last?
- How much mercy should we show others who are not doing their job?
- Are we consumed with compassion and gentleness for our fellow employees?

It is an essential question. We are asked it all the time. What do you do [for a living]? We have our elevator speech. We rehearsed and out it comes. I do X. My title is ABC. I work for XYZ company.

- Many of us have a very tactical understanding of our profession. Is it focused on the Jesus way?
- I am a doctor, CPA, lawyer, carpenter, etc. Really? That is, it?
- Jesus challenges us to see thing from His perspective.
- Jesus challenges us to understand why we are working.
- We are working to serve others and fulfill the glory of God.

As we express our faith at work, we will dive deep into what the perspective is of how Jesus sees things. It is not what we think. The Way of Jesus is different. The Way of Jesus fulfills the way God created things and brings about his glory. Our profession should be a thing of beauty, stunning everyone who sees it. Grace, love, and kindness should flow off us onto everyone we meet. They should think, I want what they have. That is a real profession. That is motivating. That is inspiring.

The "Jesus Way" goal for our faith at work: Jesus wants us to know that our profession is be **servants at work**. That is, it. That is all there is to it. It is expressed in tangible love.

Here is an example of a deeper dive in how faith at work gets manifested: Jesus is clear that our mission of faith at work is to love God with our whole being and to love our co-workers like we love ourselves. One of the characteristics of love is patience. Love is always patient. Love does not get frustrated with others.

- Is there a co-worker we will work with today that we show patience?
- Is there an opportunity to show more patience and understanding with our boss?
- How can we go out of our way to be more patient?

An insistence on one's own schedule is selfish, and it is opposed to godly love. Patient endurance and long-suffering are hallmarks of a loving character with our co-workers. Love melts away the impatience and frustration that so often hamper one's dealings with others. When the object of one's love fails or disappoints in some way, what is the proper response? According to 1 Corinthians 13:4, the loving response is patience. That is "faith at work."

Online Version: What is your profession? What do you do for a living? | Digital Business (wordpress.com)

5.1 How can "what is your profession" be answered the Jesus Way?

The way I see it: Our foundation for how we see how to express our faith at work must be solidly based on the mission given us by Jesus. Jesus is clear. _**"Many who are first will be last, and the last first."**_ Our job is to serve others. That is, it. We do it to be loving to our co-workers. There is a lot to understand about that. Jesus will help us to learn.

Why it matters: We are not just making a living for our families. We are to be making disciples for Jesus. We are to be teaching our co-workers all that Jesus commands us.

Some people have a profound sense of what their profession is all about. This is one of my favorite ways to answer the question "what is your profession." In the movie "300", King Leonidas of Sparta encounters Daxos is on the way to fight the Persian "God-King" Xerxes. They meet up along the trails.

> _**Daxos**: We heard Sparta was on the warpath and we were eager to join forces._
>
> _**King Leonidas:** If it is blood, you look for, you are welcome to join us._
>
> _**Daxos**: But you bring only this handful of soldiers against Xerxes? I see I was wrong to expect Sparta's commitment to at least match our own._
>
> _**King Leonidas:** Doesn't it? You, there. What is your profession?_
>
> _**Answer:** I am a potter, sir._
>
> _**King Leonidas:** And you, Arcadian. What is your profession?_
>
> _**Answer:** Sculptor, sir._
>
> _**King Leonidas:** And you?_
>
> _**Answer:** Blacksmith._
>
> _**King Leonidas:** Spartans! What is your profession?_
>
> _**Spartan fighters in unison:** Raising their spears 3 times and shouting a war cry each time. "Hoo! Hoo! Hoo!"_

It is worth watching the short clip here: 300 - Spartans, What Is Your Profession!?! [1080p - 60FPS] - YouTube

The Spartans knew their profession. They were not potters and sculptors. They were warriors. They had been trained to fight since their youth. That is all they knew.

__When male Spartans began military training at age seven, they would enter the agoge system__. The agoge was designed to encourage discipline and physical toughness and to emphasize the importance of the Spartan state.

__The boys lived in communal messes__ and, according to Xenophon, whose sons attended the agoge, the boys were fed "just the right amount for them never to become sluggish through being too full, while also giving them a taste of what it is not to have enough. In addition, they were trained to survive in times of privation, even if it meant stealing.

__Besides physical and weapons training,__ boys studied reading, writing, music, and dancing. Special punishments were imposed if boys did not answer questions sufficiently 'laconically' (i.e., briefly, and wittily).

Source: Wikipedia

Another example from Gideon.

Consider this from Gideon. Gideon (whose name means "Destroyer" or "Mighty Warrior") was called by Yahweh to free the people of Israel from the Midianites. Gideon saw himself as a judge of the people. God saw him as a **"Mighty Warrior."**

By God's command, Gideon took with him just 300 men whom he chose using a simple test: when the troops stopped to drink from a river, he watched to see who stuck their faces in the water and drank directly from the river (taking their eyes off what was going on around them), and who drank by cupping the water with their hand and lifting it to their mouths (leaving their eyes free to scan the environment). He picked the latter to be his warriors.

Gideon led his 300 men into the Midianite camp carrying horns and torches concealed in a clay jar (these were Molotov cocktails). At his command, the men blew their horns, threw down their torches, and shouted: ***"The sword of Yahweh and of Gideon!"***

The main thing as we consider our profession: We are in a battle. The lives of our co-workers are stake. Our mission is to serve others and we are to fight the good fight. Paul understood this in saying *"For we do not wrestle against flesh and blood, but against the rulers, against the authorities, against the cosmic powers over this present darkness, against the spiritual forces of evil in the heavenly places."* (Ephesians 6:12)

Here is the context of what Paul has to say in Ephesians 6. It is important as we live out the life of faith at work. Our service to our co-workers will be a battle some days. We need to be strong. We need the whole armor of God.

> Finally, **_be strong in the Lord_** and in the strength of his might. [11] **_Put on the whole armor of God_**, that you may be able to stand against the schemes of the devil. [12] For we do not wrestle against flesh and blood, but against the rulers, against the authorities, against the cosmic powers over this present darkness, against the spiritual forces of evil in the heavenly places. [13] Therefore take up the whole armor of God, that you may be able to withstand in the evil day, and **_having done all, to stand firm_**. [14] Stand therefore, having fastened on the belt of **_truth_**, and having put on the breastplate of **_righteousness_**, [15] and, as shoes for your feet, having put on the readiness given by the gospel of **_peace_**. [16] In all circumstances take up the shield of **_faith_**, with which you can extinguish all the flaming darts of the evil one; [17] and take the helmet of **_salvation_**, and the sword of the Spirit, which is **_the word of God_**, [18] praying at all times in the Spirit, with all prayer and supplication. To that end, keep alert with all **_perseverance_**, making supplication for all the saints, [19] and also for me, that words may be given to me in opening my mouth **_boldly to proclaim_** the mystery of the gospel, [20] for which I am an ambassador in chains, that I may declare it **_boldly_**, as I ought to speak.

"Any of you who does not give up everything he has cannot be my disciple."

(Luke 14:33).

This is the Way of Jesus. This is what Jesus thinks of leadership. We are not to regard ourselves as the greatest. Our employers may want us to see ourselves that way. Jesus knows better. We are not to lord it over others. A leader is one who serves. That is, it.

- Does Jesus want us to be leaders at work?
- Are we to spend our time working on improving our leadership skills?
- Nope! Not at all. We are to focus on learning how to serve and to love. That is, it!

Online Version: When we follow the Way of Jesus, what about leadership? Is leadership a profession?

6 THE LEADERSHIP PARADOX

6.1 WHAT IS THE PARADOX OF THE WAY OF JESUS, FAITH AT WORK AND LEADERSHIP?

Much has been written on leadership. Little has been written about faith at work. Book after book after book teaches about leadership. Recently there has been a trend to talk about "servant leadership" under the premise that is the way Jesus would have us lead.

That is a paradox. Jesus did not teach that. Jesus taught something entirely different.

It is God who places us in a position of leadership because we have a servant's heart and place ourselves last. Our goal is not to lead. Our goal is not to be first. Our Goal is always to serve.

The "Jesus Way" goal for our faith at work: Jesus has in mind for us to be humble and to serve others at work. Jesus wants us to follow him and his lead. Jesus clearly showed us it is all about service. That is all it is about. Jesus is not training leaders. Jesus is training servants. We are to follow his lead and in our discipling of others, train them to be servants as well.

> "A paradox is "a statement or proposition that, despite sound (or apparently sound) reasoning from acceptable premises, leads to a conclusion that seems senseless, logically unacceptable, or self-contradictory."

Source: PARADOX English Definition and Meaning | Lexico.com

The way I see it: There is no such thing as a servant leader. It does not exist in the reign of God where Jesus is in complete control. Our mission, given to us by Jesus is to live out our faith at work. Our goal is not to lead. Our goal is not to be first. Our Goal is to always serve.

Why it matters: Our focus matters. If we see being a servant as a pathway to leadership, then we are focused on the wrong thing. The end game is about service always. Any other way leads to the dangerous world of hypocrisy. People will see that the only reason we are doing something is to get something for ourselves. That type of motive is transparent. That type of motive makes us hypocrites.

The broad view: God wants us to do amazing, beautiful work. In the example in Exodus below, God does not want us design junk jewelry.

- God wants us to design artistic works.
- To make this happen, God gives us his Spirit.
- God gives wisdom.

- God gives us understanding.
- God gives us ability.

> The LORD also spoke to Moses: "Look, I have appointed by name Bezalel son of Uri, son of Hur, of the tribe of Judah. **_I have filled him with God's Spirit, with wisdom, understanding, and ability in every craft to design artistic works in gold, silver, and bronze, to cut gemstones for mounting, and to carve wood for work in every craft_**.

Exodus 31:1–6 (CSB)

Good news: God cares about us, and God cares about our work. By fulfilling his glory, we get his bountiful worth of satisfaction in doing a wonderful job. It is not about the work. It is about his glory.

Online Version: <u>What is the paradox of the Way of Jesus, faith at work and leadership?</u>

6.2 THE FAITH AT WORK PARADOX ACCORDING TO JESUS

Why it matters: How we see our role makes an enormous difference. It becomes a worldview of sorts. It is lens that clarifies our minute-by-minute functioning. We need to get it right. Jesus demands no less.

Here is how Jesus frames our role. It is not what we think. We are not to be first, even as servant leaders. We are always to be last. We are not training to be leaders. We are training to learn how to serve others. All the time. Every day. Every hour. That is, it. That is the main thing about the main thing. That is how we live out our faith at work.

> When they received their pay, **they began to complain** to the landowner: 'These last men put in one hour, and you made them equal to us who bore the burden of the day's work and the burning heat.'
>
> "He replied to one of them, 'Friend, I am doing you no wrong. Didn't you agree with me on a denarius? Take what is yours and go. I want to give this last man the same as I gave you. Don't I have the right to do what I want with what is mine? Are you jealous because I am generous?' **"So, the last will be first, and the first last."**

Matthew 20:11-16

And here it is again from Jesus in another context. Peter has a sense of entitlement. He frames it as a question, but his intent is clear.

> Then Peter responded to him, "See, we have left everything and followed you. So, what will there be for us?"
>
> Jesus said to them, "Truly I tell you, in the renewal of all things, when the Son of Man sits on his glorious throne, you who have followed me will also sit on twelve thrones, judging the twelve tribes of Israel. And everyone who has left houses or brothers or sisters or father or mother or children or fields because of my name will receive a hundred times more and will inherit eternal life. **But many who are first will be last, and the last first.**

Matthew 19:27-30

Jesus is clear. Here James and John want special treatment. Our role is to be servants and slaves. Note, no talk of being leaders or servant-leaders.

> When the ten disciples heard this, they became indignant with the two brothers. Jesus called them over and said, "You know that the

*rulers of the Gentiles lord it over them, and those in high positions act as tyrants over them. It must not be like that among you. On the contrary, **whoever wants to become great among you must be your servant**, and **whoever wants to be first among you must be your slave**; just as the Son of Man did not come to be served, but to serve, and to give his life as a ransom for many."*

Matthew 20:25-28

This story in Luke may be the decisive factor. Who is the greatest, the disciples wanted to know? It is the servant. Not a "servant leader." A leader is the one who serves. A leader is always last. That is the Way of Jesus.

A dispute also arose among them, as to which of them was to be regarded as the greatest. *And he said to them, "The kings of the Gentiles exercise lordship over them, and those in authority over them are called benefactors. **But not so with you**. Rather, let the greatest among you become the youngest, and **the leader as one who serves.** For whom is the greater, one who reclines at table or one who serves? Is it not the one who reclines at table? But **I am among you as the one who serves.***

Luke 22:24-30

From the example of Jesus himself. Jesus becomes the servant.

*When Jesus had <u>washed their feet </u>and put on his outer clothing, he reclined again and said to them, "Do you know what I have done for you? You call me Teacher and Master—and you are speaking rightly, since that is what I am. So, if I, your Master, and Teacher, have washed your feet, you also ought to wash one another's feet. For I have given you an example, that <u>you also should do just as I have done for you.</u> **"Truly I tell you, a servant is not greater than his master, and a messenger is not greater than the one who sent him.** If you know these things, you are happy [blessed] if you do them.*

John 13:12-17

No one, in the Way of Jesus, is to be called a leader.

*"But you are not to be called 'Rabbi,' [leader] because you have one Teacher, and you are all brothers and sisters. Do not call anyone on earth your father, because you have one Father, who is in heaven. You are not to be called instructors [leaders] either, because you have one Instructor, the Messiah. **The greatest among you will***

be your servant. Whoever exalts himself will be humbled, and whoever humbles himself will be exalted.

The "Jesus Way" goal for our faith at work: Our goal, given to us by Jesus, is to be a faithful and wise servant. If we are fortunate to manage others, our goal, at work, is to serve them. We get to serve our boss and co-workers. That is how we show our love at work.

"Who then is a faithful and wise servant, whom his master has put in charge of his household, to give them food at the proper time? 46 Happy is that servant whom the master finds doing his job when he comes. 47 Truly I tell you; he will put him in charge of all his possessions. 48 But if that wicked servant says in his heart, 'My master is delayed,' 49 and starts to beat his fellow servants, and eats and drinks with drunkards, 50 that servant's master will come on a day he does not expect him and at an hour he does not know. 51 He will cut him to pieces and assign him a place with the hypocrites, where there will be weeping and gnashing of teeth.

Matthew 24:45-51

Good news: Jesus has expectations for us in our work, it is one of being servants. We get to make decisions. We can decide to follow the way of Jesus at work and serve others or not. Jesus gives us the power of the Holy Spirit at work to serve. Jesus teaches the way of humility at work. Jesus shows us the way of kindness and mercy.

*"The man who had received one talent also approached and said, 'Master, I know you. You are a harsh man, reaping where you have not sown and gathering where you have not scattered seed. So, I was afraid and went off and hid your talent in the ground. See, you have what is yours.' "His master replied to him, '**You evil, lazy servant! If you knew that I reap where I have not sown and gather where I have not scattered, then you should have** deposited my money with the bankers, and I would have received my money back with interest when I returned. "'So, take the talent from him and give it to the one who has ten talents. **For everyone who has, more will be given, and he will have more than enough. But from the one who does not have, even what he has will be taken away from him.** And throw this worthless servant into the outer darkness, where there will be weeping and gnashing of teeth.'*

Matthew 25:14-30

Online Version: The faith at work paradox according to Jesus | Digital Business (wordpress.com)

6.3 THE STORY OF JOSEPH AS AN EXAMPLE OF FAITH AT WORK.

Why it matters: Joseph's story presents amazing insight into how God's sovereignty works to overcome evil and bring about His plan. Joseph was the eleventh son of Jacob, his first son through his favored wife, Rachel. After the announcement of his birth, we see Joseph next as a seventeen-year-old returning from shepherding the flock with his half-brothers to give Jacob a bad report of them. We are also told that Jacob "loved Joseph more than any of his other sons, because he had been born to him in his old age; and he made an ornate robe for him" (Genesis 37:3).

Joseph's brothers knew their father loved Joseph more than them, which caused them to hate him.

- To make matters worse, Joseph began relating his dreams to the family— prophetic visions showing Joseph one day ruling over his family.
- Joseph was sold by his brothers to Egyptians as a slave and served in the house of Potiphar for a long time.
- He toiled away as a slave.

Potiphar put him in prison. In jail, Joseph was again blessed by God. One day the king summoned Joseph and related his dreams. Based on Pharaoh's dreams, Joseph predicted seven years of bountiful harvests followed by seven years of severe famine in Egypt and recommended that the king begin storing grain in preparation for the coming dearth. For his wisdom, Joseph was made a ruler in Egypt, second only to the king. Joseph oversaw storing up food during the years of plenty and selling it to Egyptians and foreigners during the years of famine.

- After all his ordeals, Joseph was able to see God's hand at work.
- Yes, he was a slave. Being last, God made him first.
- As he revealed his identity to his brothers, Joseph spoke of their sin this way: "Do not be distressed and do not be angry with yourselves for selling me here, because it was to save lives that God sent me ahead of you. . .. It was not you who sent me here, but God" (Genesis 45:5, 8).
- Man's most wicked intentions can never thwart the perfect plan of God.

> *"As for you, **you meant evil against me, but God meant it for good**, to bring it about that many people should be kept alive, as they are today."*

Genesis 50:20

The "Jesus Way" goal for our faith at work: The goal is to be a servant. We are to be last. We must be comfortable with that. Jesus never stopped being a servant. Jesus went as far as to die for us. Jesus knows, just like with Joseph, that when we are last, we will be first.

God is God: God is in control of what goes on at work. Jesus has won the victory. Satan has no control. None whatsoever.

Good news: Others at work may mean evil to us. It will happen. We will be persecuted for our faith at work. We must act from a place of love and an understanding that God will use it for our good. God is in a good mood.

Online Version: The story of Joseph as an example of faith at work. | Digital Business (wordpress.com)

6.4 JESUS EXPLAINS IT TO US CLEARLY. WE ARE NOT LEADERS!

If I had to choose one text or concept that outlined Jesus' teaching on leadership, I would point to Mark 10:35-45, when James and John asked Jesus to sit at his right and left in glory.

What Jesus says in Mark 10 contradicts many popular resources on leadership available in North America today, even some leadership books with a "Christian" slant.

> And James and John, the sons of Zebedee, came up to him and said to him, "Teacher, we want you to do for us whatever we ask of you." [36] And he said to them, "What do you want me to do for you?" [37] And they said to him, **"Grant us to sit, one at your right hand and one at your left, in your glory."** [38] Jesus said to them, "You do not know what you are asking. Are you able to drink the cup that I drink, or to be baptized with the baptism with which I am baptized?" [39] And they said to him, "We are able." And Jesus said to them, "The cup that I drink you will drink, and with the baptism with which I am baptized, you will be baptized, [40] but to sit at my right hand or at my left is not mine to grant, but it is for those for whom it has been prepared." [41] And when the ten heard it, they began to be indignant at James and John. [42] And Jesus called them to him and said to them, **"You know that those who are considered rulers of the Gentiles lord it over them, and their great one's exercise authority over them. [43] But it shall not be so among you. But whoever would be great among you must be your servant, [44] and whoever would be first among you must be slave of all. [45] For even the Son of Man came not to be served but to serve, and to give his life as a ransom for many."** [34]

Source: Mark 10:35–45

The setting: Two disciples, John and James, approach Jesus privately for privileged positions of power. Some may approve of their initiative—after all, if you do not ask, you will not get it.

Their request comes on the heels of Jesus' pronouncement (for the third time) of his impending arrest, torture, and death by crucifixion. The "leaders" in Jerusalem – both Roman and Jewish – will direct these unjust and gruesome actions. We should not

---

[34] *The Holy Bible: English Standard Version*. (2016). (Mk 10:35–45). Wheaton, IL: Crossway Bibles.

forget that Jesus also declares he will be raised to life—the resurrection—which trumps the best efforts of the political, military, and religious "leaders."

Jesus is blunt with them. **"You do not know what you are asking."** Uh Oh! We just stepped in it they must be thinking. But they press on, nonetheless. If we go to Jesus and ask to be a leader, he has a blunt answer for us as well.

Jesus asks the two brothers questions, and they press back with a can-do response (another laudable attitude in modern leadership material).

When the other disciples find out about this private audience, they are indignant with James and John. The others were expressing their displeasure at having been outmaneuvered.

My conclusion is that none of them 'got it.' They did not understand true leadership.

The dominant model: Jesus features the leadership model of Romans, Greeks, and about everyone else throughout history—even in our here and now. The Master Jesus lays it out for us in Mark 10:42 (NIV): "You know that those who are regarded as rulers of the Gentiles lord it over them, and their high officials [in Greek, *megas*] exercise authority over them."

One commentary puts it in these terms: "they throw their weight around, and they ... play the tyrant."

This model can be dressed in the clothes of a benefactor: "I load this burden on you and boss you around for your benefit; I do it for your own good." And so, these leaders combine power and position and accumulate wealth and status. Sound familiar?

It is not too far off from many approaches to leadership today although they may be camouflaged or soft-pedaled.

What does Jesus teach in its place?

3 steps toward leadership—Jesus' way

Jesus presents true leadership in three steps.

First, the dominant leadership model is disqualified. Jesus states: "Not so with you" (NIV), or "among you it will be different" (NLT).

Any model of so-called leadership that advocates the use of power over, control over, manipulation of, or domination exposes itself for what it is.

Second, he tells them how his way of leading is different (Mark 10:43-44): "Whoever wants to become great [*megas*] among you must be your servant [*diakonos*], and whoever wants to be first must be slave [*doulos*] of all.

Jesus turns the dominant model on its head. Within the dominant model, the great (the *megas*) exercise authority over. Within the way of Jesus, the great (the *megas*) "must be your servant."

He adds that a person who leads in the Jesus way is not just a servant (*diakonos*), but a slave (*doulos*).

R. C. Trench writes that a *doulos* is "one that is in a permanent relation of servitude to another, his will altogether swallow up in the will of the other. He is a slave." This is not a temporary condition until leadership is secure; it is not a figurative statement as if he does not mean what he says.

Third, what does true leadership look like? Jesus not only tells us, but he also shows us. Jesus is the ultimate example (Mark 10:45): "For even the Son of Man did not come to be served, but to serve, and to give his life as a ransom for many."

A true leader not only serves those being led, but the degree of such service is also self-sacrifice. In Jesus' case, it led to his death by crucifixion on behalf of others.

3 practical observations

Here are three observations about Jesus' core teaching on leadership.

1. When our question is "Who is the greatest?"—we do not get it. This may be spoken or unspoken. It manifests itself in many ways. Jesus is not going to answer this question. Rather, he is asking the crucial question: "Who is serving?"
2. Elsewhere Jesus says to his disciples, "You are not greater [*megas*] than me" (John 13:16). If a person is looking to be great that person does not understand his or her relationship to the Master Jesus well, or at all. Do we tend to domesticate or tame what Jesus is saying? A true leader is not only subject to Jesus the Messiah in mind, will, and body; a true leader is serving Jesus the Messiah by serving his people.
3. Jesus is not teaching mere theory. This is the stuff of real life. A *true* leader is called to be serving those that are led. It is dynamic, effective, and real.

If you are not a little frightened by what Jesus is saying about *true* leadership—you do not get it.

The "Jesus Way" goal for our faith at work: Jesus is not looking for leaders. Jesus is looking for servants and obedient ones at that. Jesus wants us to follow the Way of Love. Will we?

Online Version: Jesus Explains it to us clearly. We are not leaders! | Digital Business (wordpress.com)

7 KEY THEMES – JESUS MANIFESTO

7.1 FIVE FOCUS AREAS FOR FAITH AT WORK.

Here are five focus areas for consideration that will make a difference for our faith at work.

1. **Love is the main thing about the main thing.** We cannot go wrong if our mission every day is to focus on love. It should be our passion and mission at work.
2. **Humility always wins the day**. Even evil people at work appreciate the value of humility. Ours is true humility based on our understanding of human nature and our own sins and mistakes. We admit them, repent, and seek mercy from Jesus.
3. **Mercy is real and necessary.** Being people of mercy will separate us from others at work. Mercy will show our love.
4. **Purity is important and not to be ignored.** Our actions must always reflect purity and a right standing with God.
5. **Peacemaking changes everything.** We should always, in our humility and mercy, be advocates for peace.

Here is the whole list from Jesus. Jesus is serious that he wants us to show others the Way of Jesus as we work these out at work.

- Fortunate [blessed] are the **poor in spirit**, for the kingdom of heaven is theirs.
- Fortunate are those who **mourn**, for they will be comforted.
- Fortunate are the **humble**, for they will inherit the earth.
- Fortunate are those who **hunger and thirst for righteousness**, for they will be filled.
- Fortunate are the **merciful**, for they will be shown mercy.
- Fortunate are the **pure in heart**, for they will see God.
- Fortunate are the **peacemakers**, for they will be called sons of God.
- Fortunate are those who are **persecuted because of righteousness**, for the kingdom of heaven is theirs."

We need to keep in mind that God is God. When you bundle all the attributes of God in one unified whole, you have God. God is not just one or two things. God is unlike anything or anyone we could ever know or imagine. He is one of a kind, unique and without comparison. Even describing him with mere words truly falls short of capturing who he is – our words simply cannot do justice to describe our holy God.

God is infinite, never changes, has no needs, all powerful, all-knowing, always everywhere, full of perfect, unchanging wisdom, faithful, good, just, wrathful, merciful, gracious, loving, holy, glorious, infinitely beautiful, and great and more. God is God.

Online Version: Five Focus areas for faith at work. | Digital Business (wordpress.com)

7.2 How to be fortunate and more than happy in our faith at work (the Beatitudes)

When Jesus starts His manifesto [Matthew 5-7] (aka the Sermon on the Mount), he starts with these 8 principles of how to work out our faith at work. He is speaking to disciples and not the masses. This is an important distinction.

We will look at these briefly individually but taken together they are a stunning framework for our life at work. These changes everything in our relations with co-workers, customers, bosses, partners, suppliers, and everyone we interact with at work.

The word traditionally translated "blessed" from the Greek is μακάριος **makariŏs**, *mak-ar´-ee-os*. It means happy, happier, or fortunate. We will use the word fortunate for our purposes here. [35]

- Fortunate [blessed] are the **poor in spirit**, for the kingdom of heaven is theirs.
- Fortunate are those who **mourn**, for they will be comforted.
- Fortunate are the **humble**, for they will inherit the earth.
- Fortunate are those who **hunger and thirst for righteousness**, for they will be filled.
- Fortunate are the **merciful**, for they will be shown mercy.
- Fortunate are the **pure in heart**, for they will see God.
- Fortunate are the **peacemakers**, for they will be called sons of God.
- Fortunate are those who are **persecuted because of righteousness**, for the kingdom of heaven is theirs."

The "Jesus Way" goal for our faith at work: Jesus wants us to take seriously all the principles he laid out in the beatitudes. We must focus on love at the core but work it out with mercy and humility.

The principles set forth the balanced and variegated character of Christian (disciples who follow Jesus) people at work. These are not eight separate and distinct groups of disciples, some of whom are meek, while others are merciful and yet others are called upon to endure persecution. They are eight qualities of the same group who at the same time are meek and merciful, poor in spirit and pure in heart, mourning and hungry, peacemakers and persecuted. This is a comprehensive approach from Jesus. We must consider them all at our workplace.

---

[35] Strong, J. (1996). *The New Strong's Dictionary of Hebrew and Greek Words*. Nashville: Thomas Nelson.

Further, the group showing these marks is not an elitist set, a small spiritual aristocracy remote from the common run of Christians who are disciples. On the contrary, the beatitudes are the Messiah's own specification of what every disciple ought to be. All these qualities are to characterize all his followers.

- Just as the ninefold fruit of the Spirit which Paul lists is to ripen in every Christian character, so the eight beatitudes which Jesus speaks describe his ideal for every citizen of God's kingdom.
- Unlike the gifts of the Spirit which he distributes to different members of the Messiah's body to equip them for distinct kinds of service, the same Spirit is concerned to work all these Christian graces in us all.
- There is no escape from our responsibility to covet them all.[36]

Online Version: How to be fortunate and more than happy in our faith at work (the Beatitudes). | Digital Business (wordpress.com)

---

[36] Stott, J. R. W., & Stott, J. R. W. (1985). *The message of the Sermon on the mount (Matthew 5-7): Christian counterculture* (p. 31). Leicester; Downers Grove, IL: InterVarsity Press.

7.4.1 Why should our faith at work point to being poor in spirit?

Leaders are poor in spirit.

- "**Fortunate [blessed] are the poor in spirit, for theirs is the kingdom of heaven**." Matthew 5:3 – The Jesus Manifesto
- "**Fortunate [blessed] are you who are poor, because the kingdom of God is yours.**" Luke 6:20 – Sermon on the Plain
- "But **woe to you who are rich, for you have received your comfort.**" Luke 6:24 – Sermon on the Plain

Some questions to think about.

- What exactly does it mean to be poor in spirit?
- Why does being poor in spirit result in the kingdom of heaven?
- Why is "poor in spirit" something God wants us to be?
- Why would God want us to be "poor" at anything?
- What, then, does it mean to be spiritually poor?

How do leaders see poverty of spirit?

- It is a sense of powerlessness in ourselves.
- It is a sense of spiritual bankruptcy and helplessness before God.
- It is a sense of moral uncleanness before God.
- It is a sense of personal unworthiness before God.
- It is a sense that if there is to be any life, joy, or usefulness, it will have to be all of God and all of grace.

Online Version: Why should our faith at work point to being poor in spirit? | Digital Business (wordpress.com)

7.4.2 What is poverty of spirit at work?

In the beatitudes of the Sermon on the Mount (what I call the Jesus Manifesto), Jesus declares, "Blessed are the poor in spirit, for theirs is the kingdom of heaven" (Matthew 5:3). What exactly does it mean to be poor in spirit, and why does being poor in spirit result in the kingdom of heaven? Why is "poor in spirit" something God wants us to be? Why would God want us to be "poor" at anything?

Some propose that Jesus is speaking of financial poverty, that He is advocating being poor so that riches and possession do not come between us and God. While it is true that Jesus elsewhere warned against seeking riches (Matthew 6:24), that does not seem to be Jesus' point in Matthew 5:3. Jesus is speaking of being "poor in spirit"; i.e., being "spiritually poor." In the beatitudes, Jesus is concerned with spiritual realities, not material possessions. What, then, does it mean to be spiritually poor?

To be poor in spirit at work is to recognize your utter spiritual bankruptcy before God. It is understanding that you have absolutely nothing of worth to offer God. Being poor in spirit is admitting that, because of your sin, you are completely destitute spiritually and can do nothing to deliver yourself from your dire situation. Jesus is saying that, no matter your status in life, you must recognize your spiritual poverty before you can come to God in faith to receive the salvation He offers.

The best later example of the same truth is the nominal church of Laodicea to whom John was directed to send a letter from the glorified Messiah. He quoted their complacent words and added his own assessment of them: 'You say, I am rich, I have prospered, and I need nothing; not knowing that you are wretched, pitiable, poor, blind, and naked.' This visible church, for all its Christian profession, was not truly Christian at all. Self-satisfied and superficial, it was composed (according to Jesus) of blind and naked beggars. But the tragedy was they would not admit it. They were rich, not poor, in spirit.

Still today, as leaders, the indispensable condition of receiving the kingdom of God is to acknowledge our spiritual poverty. God still sends the rich away empty. As C. H. Spurgeon expressed it,

> *'The way to rise in the kingdom is to sink in ourselves.'*

Why and how does being poor in spirit result in the kingdom of heaven? God offers us salvation as a gift, through the sacrifice of Jesus the Messiah on the cross, the full payment for sin's penalty. Before we can receive this gift, we must understand that we cannot make ourselves worthy of it. Salvation is by grace through faith, not of works (Ephesians 2:8-9). We must recognize our sinfulness before we can understand our need for a Savior. We must admit our spiritual poverty before we can receive the spiritual riches God offers (Ephesians 1:3). We must, in short, be "poor in spirit."

When Jesus says, "Blessed are the poor in spirit, for theirs is the kingdom of heaven," He is declaring that, before we can enter God's kingdom, we must recognize the utter worthlessness of our own spiritual currency and the inability of our own works to save us.

What is the Old Testament view of poverty of spirit? The Old Testament supplies the necessary background against which to interpret this beatitude. At first to be 'poor' meant to be in literal, material need. But gradually, because the needy had no refuge but God, 'poverty' came to have spiritual overtones and to be identified with humble dependence on God. Thus, the psalmist chose himself 'this poor man' who cried out to God in his need, 'and the Lord heard him, and saved him out of all his troubles.' The 'poor man' in the Old Testament is one who is both afflicted and unable to save himself, and who therefore looks to God for salvation, while recognizing that he has no claim upon him.

This kind of spiritual poverty is specially commended in Isaiah. It is the poor and needy', who 'seek water and there is none, and their tongue is parched with thirst', for whom God promises to 'open rivers on the bare heights, and fountains in the midst of the valleys', and to 'make the wilderness a pool of water, and the dry land springs of water'. The 'poor' are also described as people with 'a contrite and humble spirit;' to them God looks and with them (though he is 'The high and lofty One' who inhabits eternity, whose name is Holy') he is pleased to dwell.

It is to such that the Lord's anointed would proclaim good tidings of salvation, a prophecy which Jesus consciously fulfilled in the Nazareth synagogue: 'The Spirit of the Lord is upon me, because he has anointed me to preach good news to the poor.' Further, the rich tended to compromise with surrounding heathenism; it was the poor who remained faithful to God. So, wealth and worldliness, poverty and godliness went together. Thus, to be 'poor in spirit' is to acknowledge our spiritual poverty, indeed our spiritual bankruptcy, before God. For we are sinners, under the holy wrath of God, and deserving nothing but the judgment of God. We have nothing to offer, nothing to plead, nothing with which to buy the favor of heaven.

Online Version: What is poverty of spirit at work? | Digital Business (wordpress.com)

7.4.3 What do corporate leaders know about poverty of spirit?

We do not belong anywhere except alongside the publican in Jesus' parable, crying out with downcast eyes, 'God, be merciful to me a sinner!' As Calvin wrote:

> **'He only who is reduced to nothing in himself, and relies on the mercy of God, is poor in spirit.'**

To such, and only to such, the kingdom of God is given. For God's rule which brings salvation is a gift as free as it is utterly undeserved. It must be received with the dependent humility of a little child. Thus, right at the beginning of his Sermon on the Mount, Jesus contradicted all human judgments and all nationalistic expectations of the kingdom of God.

The kingdom is given to the poor, not the rich; the feeble, not the mighty; to little children humble enough to accept it, not to soldiers who boast that they can obtain it by their own prowess. In our Master's own day it was not the Pharisees who entered the kingdom, who thought they were rich, so rich in merit that they thanked God for their attainments; nor the Zealots who dreamed of establishing the kingdom by blood and sword; but publicans and prostitutes, the rejects of human society, who knew they were so poor they could offer nothing and achieve nothing. All they could do was to cry to God for mercy; and he heard their cry.

How do leaders see poverty of spirit?

- It is a sense of powerlessness in ourselves.
- It is a sense of spiritual bankruptcy and helplessness before God.
- It is a sense of moral uncleanness before God.
- It is a sense of personal unworthiness before God.
- It is a sense that if there is to be any life, joy, or usefulness, it will have to be all of God and all of grace.

Online Version: What do corporate leaders know about poverty of spirit? | Digital Business (wordpress.com)

7.4.4 Is spiritual poverty a judgement on leaders?

Here are some thought provoking scriptures on being poor in spirit.

- **Amos 8:11 (CSB) — 11** Look, the days are coming— this is the declaration of the Lord God— <u>when I will send a famine through the land: not a famine of bread or a thirst for water, but of hearing the words of the Lord.</u>
- **Psalm 51:11 (CSB) — 11** <u>Do not banish me from your presence or take your Holy Spirit from me.</u>
- **Psalm 74:9 (CSB) — 9** There are no signs for us to see. <u>There is no longer a prophet. And none of us knows how long this will last.</u>
- **Lamentations 2:9 (CSB) — 9** Zion's gates have fallen to the ground; he has destroyed and shattered the bars on her gates. Her king and her leaders live among the nations, instruction is no more, and <u>even her prophets receive no vision from the Lord.</u>
- **Ezekiel 7:26 (CSB) — 26** Disaster after disaster will come, and there will be rumor after rumor. <u>Then they will look for a vision from a prophet, but instruction will perish from the priests and counsel from the elders.</u>
- **Matthew 13:14–15 (CSB) — 14** Isaiah's prophecy is fulfilled in them, which says: <u>You will listen and listen, but never understand; you will look and look, but never perceive.</u> **15** For these people's heart has grown callous; their ears are hard of hearing, and they have shut their eyes; otherwise, they might see with their eyes, and hear with their ears, and understand with their hearts, and turn back— and I would heal them.
- **Revelation 2:5 (CSB) — 5** <u>Remember then how far you have fallen; repent and do the work you did at first.</u> Otherwise, I will come to you and remove your lampstand from its place, unless you repent.

<u>**The great leader David recognized he was poor and needy.**</u>

- **Psalm 40:17 (CSB) — 17** <u>I am oppressed and needy; may the Lord think of me.</u> You are my helper and my deliverer; my God, do not delay.
- **Psalm 34:6 (CSB) — 6** <u>This poor man cried, and the Lord heard him and saved him from all his troubles.</u>
- **Psalm 35:10 (CSB) — 10** All my bones will say, <u>"Lord, who is like you, rescuing the poor from one too strong for him, the poor or the needy from one who robs him?"</u>
- **Psalm 70:5 (CSB) — 5** <u>I am oppressed and needy; hurry to me,</u> God. You are my help and my deliverer; Lord, do not delay.
- **Psalm 86:1 (CSB) — 1** <u>Listen, Lord, and answer me, for I am poor and needy.</u>
- **Psalm 109:22 (CSB) —** <u>22 For I am suffering and needy; my heart is wounded within me.</u>

Leaders know that God will satisfy, save & accept the poor in spirit.

- **God will satisfy the poor in spirit.**
  - ○ **Matthew 5:6 (CSB) — 6 <u>Happy are those who hunger and thirst for righteousness, for they will be filled.</u>**
- **God will save the poor in spirit.**
  - ○ **Psalm 116:6 (CSB) — 6 <u>The Lord guards the inexperienced; I was helpless, and he saved me.</u>**
- **God will accept the poor in spirit.**
  - ○ **Psalm 51:17 (CSB) — 17 <u>The sacrifice pleasing to God is a broken spirit.</u>** You will not despise a broken and humbled heart, God.
  - ○ **Isaiah 66:2 (CSB) — 2** My hand made all these things, and so they all came into being. This is the Lord's declaration<u>**. I will look favorably on this kind of person: one who is humble, submissive in spirit, and trembles at my word.**</u>

Online Version: Is spiritual poverty a judgement on leaders at work? | Digital Business (wordpress.com)

7.4.5 Do corporate leaders understand that God will be close and hear the prayers of the poor in spirit?

- **God will be close to the poor in spirit at work.**
    - **Psalm 34:18 (CSB) — 18** Yahweh is near the brokenhearted; he saves those crushed in spirit.
    - **Isaiah 57:15 (CSB) — 15** For the High and Exalted One, who lives forever, whose name is holy, says this: "I live in a high and holy place, and with the oppressed and lowly of spirit, to revive the spirit of the lowly and revive the heart of the oppressed.
- **God will hear the prayers of employees who poor in spirit.**
    - **Psalm 102:17 (CSB) — 17** He will pay attention to the prayer of the destitute and will not despise their prayer.

God will meet the needs of the poor in spirit.

- **Isaiah 61:1 (CSB) — 1** The Spirit of the Lord God is on me, because the Lord has anointed me to bring good news to the poor. He has sent me to heal the brokenhearted, to proclaim liberty to the captives and freedom to the prisoners.
- **Luke 1:53 (CSB) — 53** He has satisfied the hungry with good things and sent the rich away empty. ~Mother May in the Magnificat.

The "Jesus Way" goal for our faith at work: We need to reflect to others our understanding that God is God. When you bundle all the attributes of God in one unified whole, you have God. God is not just one or two things. God is unlike anything or anyone we could ever know or imagine. He is one of a kind, unique and without comparison. Even describing him with mere words truly falls short of capturing who he is – our words simply cannot do justice to describe our holy God.

God will give grace to the poor in spirit.

- **James 4:6 (CSB) — 6** But he gives greater grace. Therefore, he says: <u>**God resists the proud, but gives grace to the humble.**</u>
- **James 4:10 (CSB) — 10** <u>**Humble yourselves before the Lord, and he will exalt you.**</u>
- **1 Peter 5:5–6 (CSB) — 5** In the same way, you who are younger, be subject to the elders. <u>**All of you clothe yourselves with humility toward one another because God resists the proud but gives grace to the humble.**</u> **6** Humble yourselves, therefore, under the mighty hand of God, so that he may exalt you at the proper time,
- **Proverbs 3:34 (CSB) — 34** <u>**He mocks those who mock but gives grace to the humble.**</u>

Leaders know how to become poor so others can become rich.

> *For you know the grace of our Master Jesus the Messiah, that though He was rich, **yet for your sake He became poor, so that you through His poverty might become rich**.*

2 Corinthians 8:9

Thus, Jesus was born into a family that was part of the lower economic class. We see this material status has not changed 30 years later, during Jesus' earthly ministry. Jesus' comments on his own economic status, such as when he said, "Foxes have holes, and birds of the air have nests, but the Son of Man has nowhere to lay his head" (Matthew 8:20). The good news narratives bear out this testimony.

Jesus had extraordinarily little by way of material possessions during his ministry.

Consider the following: Jesus…

- ➤ preached from borrowed boats,
- ➤ multiplied borrowed food,
- ➤ rode on a borrowed colt,
- ➤ and was buried in a borrowed tomb.

Where does money come from?

- "But you shall remember the Master your God; for it is He that gives you power to get wealth" (Deut. 8:18).
- Instruct those who are rich in the present age not to be arrogant or to set their hope on the uncertainty of wealth, but on God, who richly provides us with all things to enjoy. (1 Timothy 6:17)

I must be careful not to fall into the trap that anything I have is the result of something I have done. It is a dangerous way to think and Jesus challenges me to change my mind about that. Thinking and acting that way causes me to miss God's goal for my life. I am getting clear on that.

If wealth makes a person proud, then he understands neither himself nor his wealth. "But you shall remember the Master your God; for it is He that gives you power to get wealth" (Deut. 8:18). We are not owners; we are stewards. If we have wealth, it is by the goodness of God and not because of any special merits on our part. The possessing of material wealth ought to humble a person and cause him to glorify God, not himself.

It is possible to be "rich in the world [age]" (1 Tim. 6:17) and be poor in the next. It is also possible to be poor in this world and rich in the next. Jesus talked about both. But a believer can be rich in this world and rich in the next if he uses what he must honor God. In fact, a person who is poor in this world can use even his limited means to glorify God and discover great reward in the next world.

Trust God, not wealth. The rich farmer in our Master's parable thought that his wealth meant security, when really it was evidence of insecurity. He was not really trusting God.

Riches are uncertain, not only in their value (which changes constantly), but also in their durability. Thieves can steal wealth, investments can drop in value, and the ravages of time can ruin houses and cars. If God gives us wealth, we should trust Him, the Giver, and not the gifts.

Enjoy what God gives you. Yes, the word enjoy is in the Bible! In fact, one of the recurring themes in Ecclesiastes is, "Enjoy the blessings of life now, because life will end one day." This is not sinful "hedonism," living for the pleasures of life. It is simply enjoying all that God gives us for His glory.

Online Version: Do corporate leaders understand that God will be close and hear the prayers of the poor in spirit? | Digital Business (wordpress.com)

7.4.6 Leaders know how not to fall into the temptation to become rich.

"People who want to get rich fall into temptation and a trap and into many foolish and harmful desires that plunge men into ruin and destruction. For the love of money is the root of all kinds of evil. Some people, eager for money, have wandered from the faith and pierced themselves with many griefs."

(1 Timothy 6:9–10).

People are more important than money. Therefore, if you are offering your gift at the altar and remember that your brother has something against you, leave your gift there in front of the altar. First go and be reconciled with your brother; then come and offer your gift. — Matthew 5:23-24.

At work we give to those who are needy

Give to the one who asks you, *and do not turn away from the one who wants to borrow from you.*

Matthew 5:42

*"**If anyone has material possessions and sees his brother in need but has no pity on him, how can the love of God be in him?** Dear children, let us not love with words or tongue but with action and in truth."*

(1 John 3:17–18)

Interesting question: How can you give if you do not have money?

Disciples of Jesus give in secret. But when you give to the needy, do not announce it with trumpets, as the hypocrites do in the synagogues and on the streets, to be honored by men. I tell you the truth, they have received their reward in full. But when you give to the needy, do not let your left hand know what your right hand is doing, so that your giving may be in secret. Then your Father, who sees what is done in secret, will reward you. — Matthew 6:2-4

Disciple of Jesus invest in the spiritual not monetary. Do not store up for yourselves treasures on earth, where moth and rust destroy, and where thieves break in and steal. But store up for yourselves treasures in heaven, where moth and rust do not destroy, and where thieves do not break in and steal. For where your treasure is, there your heart will be also. — Matthew 6:19-21

God and money. No one can serve two masters. Either he will hate the one and love the other, or he will be devoted to the one and despise the other. You cannot serve both God and Money. —Matthew 6:24

The "Jesus Way" goal for our faith at work: Jesus wants us focus on the reign of God and not materialism. Life is more than the next promotion. We need to act that way.

Online Version: Leaders know how not to fall into the temptation to become rich. | Digital Business (wordpress.com)

7.4.7 What do leaders worry about at work?

The "Jesus Way" goal for our faith at work: Jesus wants us to trust God and not be anxious or worry. That is truly clear. Our faith at work requires us not to be anxious. Our colleagues will see that and respect that.

> Therefore, I tell you, **do not worry about your life**, what you will eat or drink; or about your body, what you will wear. Is life not more important than food, and the body more important than clothes? Look at the birds of the air; they do not sow or reap or store away in barns, and yet your heavenly Father feeds them. Are you not much more valuable than they are? Who among you, by worrying, can add a single hour to his life?
>
> And why do you worry about **clothes**? See how the lilies of the field grow. They do not labor or spin. Yet I tell you that not even Solomon in all his splendor was dressed like one of these. If that is how God clothes the grass of the field, which is here today and tomorrow is thrown into the fire, will he not much more clothe you, O you of little faith? So do not worry, saying, 'What shall we **eat**?' or 'What shall we **drink**?' or 'what shall we **wear**?' For the pagans run after all these things, and your heavenly Father knows that you need them. But **seek first his kingdom and his righteousness**, and all these things will be given to you as well. Therefore, do not worry about tomorrow, for tomorrow will worry about itself. Each day has enough trouble of its own.

Matthew 6:25-34

- **Leaders give freely:** Freely you have received, freely give. Do not take along any gold or silver or copper in your belts; take no bag for the journey, or extra tunic, or sandals or a staff; for the worker is worth his keeping. — Matthew 10:8b-10
- **Is wealth deceitful?** Now the one sown among the thorns—this is one who hears the word, but the worries of this age and the deceitfulness of wealth choke the word, and it becomes unfruitful. Matthew 13:22
- **What is God's kingdom like?** The kingdom of heaven is like a treasure hidden in a field. When a man found it, he hid it again, and then in his joy he went and sold all he had and bought that field.
- Again, the kingdom of heaven is like a merchant looking for fine pearls. When he found one of terrific value. he went away and sold everything he had and bought it. — Matthew 13:44-46

Leaders understand the value of giving.

Now a man came up to Jesus and asked, "Teacher, what good thing must I do to get eternal life?"

"Why do you ask me about what is good?" Jesus replied. "There is only One who is good. If you want to enter life, obey the commandments." "Which ones?" the man inquired. Jesus replied,

"'Do not murder, do not commit adultery, do not steal, do not give false testimony, honor your father and mother,' and 'love your neighbor as yourself.'"

"All these I have kept," the young man said. "What do I still lack?"

*Jesus answered, **"If you want to be perfect, go, sell your possessions, and give to the poor, and you will have treasure in heaven. Then come, follow me."***

When the young man heard his, he went away sad, because he had great wealth. —

Matthew 19:16-22

Can the rich enter the Kingdom of God?

*Then Jesus said to his disciples, "I tell you the truth, it is hard for a rich man to enter the kingdom of heaven. Again, I tell you, **it is easier for a camel to go through the eye of a needle than for a rich man to enter the kingdom of God."***

When the disciples heard this, they were astonished and asked, "Who then can be saved?"

Jesus looked at them and said, "With man this is impossible, but with God all things are possible."

Matthew 19:23-26

Peter answered him, "We have left everything to follow you! What will there be for us?"

*Jesus said to them, "I tell you the truth, at the renewal of all things, when the Son of Man sits on his glorious throne, you who have followed me will also sit on twelve thrones, judging the twelve tribes of Israel. And everyone who has left houses or brothers or sisters or father or mother or children or fields for my sake **will receive a***

hundred times as much and will inherit eternal life. But many who
are first will be last, and the last first." — Matthew 19:23-30

Leaders give to those in need.

Then the King will say to those on his right, 'Come, you who are
blessed by my Father; inherit the kingdom prepared for you from the
foundation of the world.

*"'For I was hungry and you gave me something to eat; I was
thirsty and you gave me something to drink; I was a stranger
and you took me in; I was naked and you clothed me; I was sick
and you took care of me; I was in prison and you visited me.'*

"Then the righteous will answer him, 'Lord, when did we see you
hungry and feed you, or thirsty and give you something to drink?
When did we see you with a stranger and take you in, or without
clothes and clothe you? When did we see you sick, or in prison, and
visit you?'

"And the King will answer them, 'Truly I tell you, whatever you did for
one of the least of these brothers and sisters of mine, you did for me.'

Giving to the poor or giving to Jesus

While Jesus was in Bethany in the home of a man known as Simon
the Leper, a woman came to him with an alabaster jar of awfully
expensive perfume, which she poured on his head as he was
reclining at the table.

When the disciples saw this, they were indignant.

"Why this waste?" they asked. "This perfume could have been sold at
a high price and **the money given to the poor**."

Aware of this, Jesus said to them,

"Why are you bothering this woman? She has done a beautiful thing
for me. **The poor you will always have with you**, but you will not
always have me. When she poured this perfume on my body, she did
it to prepare me for burial. I tell you the truth, wherever this good
news is preached throughout the world, what she has done will also
be told, in memory of her."

Matthew 26:6-13

Online Version: <u>What do leaders worry about at work? | Digital Business (wordpress.com)</u>

7.4.8 Do leaders know what we are working for?

The "Jesus Way" goal for our faith at work: Jesus wants us to be content with what we have. Jesus needs for us be poor in spirit. That is the way of Jesus.

> **"Do not work for the food that perishes, but for the food that endures for eternal life**, which the Son of Man will give you. For it is on him that God the Father has set his seal."

John 6:28

Working with all our heart.

> **"Whatever you do, work at it with all your heart, as working for the Master, not for human masters**, since you know that you will receive an inheritance from the Master as a reward. It is the Master the Messiah you are serving."

(Colossians 3:23–24).

Leaders understand spiritual blessings.

Ephesians 1:3 tells us, "Praise be to the God and Father of our Master Jesus the Messiah, who has blessed us in the heavenly realms with every spiritual blessing in the Messiah."

The poverty of selfishness.

> And He told them a parable, saying, "The land of a rich man was very productive. "And he began reasoning to himself, saying, 'What shall I do, since I have no place to store my crops?' "Then he said, 'This is what I will do: I will tear down my barns and build larger ones, and there I will store all my grain and my goods. 'And I will say to my soul, "Soul, you have many goods laid up for many years to come; take your ease, eat, drink and be merry."' "But God said to him, **'You fool! This very night your soul is required of you; and now who will own what you have prepared?' "So is the man who stores up treasure for himself and is not rich toward God."**

Luke 12:16–21

Leaders know how to attain all the wealth of God.

> That their hearts may be encouraged, having been knit together in love, and **attaining to all the wealth that comes from the full assurance of understanding, resulting in a true knowledge of**

> **God's mystery**, that is, the Messiah Himself, in whom are hidden all
> the treasures of wisdom and knowledge.

Colossians 2:2–3

The scope of Paul's challenges.

> 24 Five times I received at the hands of the Jews the forty lashes
> less one. 25 Three times I was beaten with rods. Once I was stoned.
> Three times I was shipwrecked; a night and a day I was adrift at
> sea; 26 on frequent journeys, in danger from rivers, danger from
> robbers, danger from my own people, danger from Gentiles, danger
> in the city, danger in the wilderness, danger at sea, danger from false
> brothers; 27 in toil and hardship, through many a sleepless night, in
> hunger and thirst, often without food, in cold and exposure. 28 And,
> apart from other things, there is the daily pressure on me of my
> anxiety for all the churches.

2 Corinthians 11:24-28

Leaders learn to be content.

> Not that I am speaking of being in need, **for I have learned in
> whatever situation I am to be content**. I know how to be brought
> low, and I know how to abound. In any and every circumstance, I
> have learned the secret of facing plenty and hunger, abundance, and
> need. I can do all things through him who strengthens me.

Philippians 4:11-13

Online Version: Do leaders know what we are working for? | Digital Business
(wordpress.com)

7.5 ARE WE READY TO MOURN AT WORK?

> ### _Blessed [fortunate] are those who mourn, for they will be comforted._ [40]

~Jesus (Matthew 5:4)

One might almost translate this second beatitude 'Happy are the unhappy' to draw attention to the startling paradox it holds. What kind of sorrow can it be which brings the joy of the Messiah's blessing to those who feel it?

- It is plain from the context that those here promised comfort are not primarily those who mourn the loss of a loved one, but those who mourn the loss of their innocence, their righteousness, their self-respect.
- It is not the sorrow of bereavement to which the Messiah refers, but the sorrow of repentance.
- Are we ready to mourn at work?
- Will we, as a person of faith, show the sorrow of our repentance?

This is the second stage of spiritual blessing for our faith at work. It is one thing to be spiritually poor and acknowledge it; it is another to grieve and to mourn over it. Or, in more theological language, confession is one thing, contrition is another.

We need, then, to see that the disciple's life at work, according to Jesus, is not all joy and laughter. Some Christians imagine that, especially if they are filled with the Spirit, they must wear a perpetual grin on their face and be continuously boisterous and bubbly. How unbiblical can one become? No. In Luke's version of the Sermon Jesus added to this beatitude a solemn woe: 'Woe to you that laugh now.' The truth is that there are such things as Christian tears, and too few of us ever weep them.

> ### _Be miserable, and mourn, and weep; let your laughter be turned into mourning, and your joy into gloom._ [10] _Humble yourselves in the presence of the Master, and He will exalt you._

---

[40] _New American Standard Bible_. (2020). (Mt 5:4). La Habra, CA: The Lockman Foundation.

Jesus wept over the sins of others. We too should weep more over the evil in the workplace, as did the godly men of biblical times.

- 'My eyes shed streams of tears,' the psalmist could say to God, 'because men do not keep your law.'
- Ezekiel heard God's faithful people described as those 'who sigh and groan over all the abominations that are committed in (Jerusalem).'
- And Paul wrote of the false teachers troubling the churches and workplaces of his day: 'Many, of whom I … now tell you **even with tears**, live as enemies of the cross of the Messiah.'

The "Jesus Way" goal for our faith at work: We must mourn at work. We must cry over the evil we see around us. Jesus compels us to go beyond empathy and have compassion on our colleagues.

Online Version: Are we ready to mourn at work? | Digital Business (wordpress.com)

---

[41] *New American Standard Bible*. (2020). (Jas 4:9–10). La Habra, CA: The Lockman Foundation.

7.6 WILL HUMILITY AT WORK WIN THE DAY?

Blessed [fortunate] are the gentle [meek/humble], for they will inherit the earth. [42]

~Jesus (Matthew 5:5)

The domineering, the aggressive, the harsh, and the tyrannical are often those who try to dominate the workplace and set up their own little kingdoms. But Jesus says that it is the "gentle" who will inherit the earth, harking back to the psalmist who encourages those who have been treated harshly by evildoers. At work, gentleness and humility will prevail.

This shifts the focus from individual personal qualities ("poor in spirit," "those who mourn") to interpersonal attributes ("the gentle"), to people who do not assert themselves over others to advance their own causes at work.

The "Jesus Way" goal for our faith at work: Jesus clearly wants us to humble, gentle and meek. That is the way of love. Our colleagues will see it and notice it. It will be more of a difference than we can ever imagine.

Meekness does not imply weakness, however, for this same term is applied to Jesus, who describes himself as "gentle and humble in heart." Jesus was not afraid to confront the religious and corporate leaders when necessary or to rebuke his own disciples for self-centeredness. Will we be strong enough to face it at work?

Jesus exemplifies best what it means to be gentle. It takes tremendous strength to bring others into God's will, but when that strength is coupled with a selfless non assertiveness, it produces a gentle person who can patiently endure much to bring about God's purposes for his people at work.

- Such gentle persons "will inherit the earth."
- Jesus assumes this gentle posture as he preaches good news, proclaims freedom, and announces the arrival of the Lord's favor, and blessed are those who do not take offence at his gentle messianic ministry.

---

[42] *New American Standard Bible*. (2020). (Mt 5:5). La Habra, CA: The Lockman Foundation.

- This points to the reign of the Messiah on this earth and work, but even now Jesus' disciples have entered their spiritual inheritance.[43]

<u>We will be out of step with the corporate cultures</u> when we pursue the way of humility and gentleness. It is a harsh workplace. We will stand out. Our filter for decisions must be different. We must be ready. We may get fired for our stance.

Online Version: <u>Will humility at work win the day? | Digital Business (wordpress.com)</u>

---

[43] Wilkins, M. J. (2004). *Matthew* (p. 207). Grand Rapids, MI: Zondervan Publishing House.

7.6.1 Can we be meek and humble at work?

> "Fortunate [Blessed] are the **_meek_**, for they shall inherit the earth.

When you get in the shoot, you know what the outcome is going to be. You will be bucked off the horse. The only question is how long it will take.
- •The only goal of the horse is to throw you off its back. It always does.
- •I have been humbled in my life. Why?
  - Mother's death
  - Fired from several jobs.
  - I really did have cancer and now have heart disease.
  - I have been homeless several times.
  - I have been extremely poor.
- •What is the good news here? Can I be happy when I am poor in spirit when I mourn? Can I be happy when I weep now?
- •Where does it lead?

πραΰτης, ητος *f*, **πραϋπαθία, ας** *f*: gentleness of attitude and behavior, in contrast with harshness in one's dealings with others—'gentleness, meekness, mildness.'

- πραΰτης: μετὰ πάσης ταπεινοφροσύνης καὶ πραΰτητος 'be always humble and meek' Eph 4:2.
- πραϋπαθία: δίωκε … ὑπομονήν, πραϋπαθίαν 'strive for … endurance and gentleness' 1 Tm 6:11.

In several languages 'gentleness' is often expressed as a negation of harshness, so that 'gentleness' may often by rendered as 'not being harsh with people,' but gentleness may also be expressed in some instances in an idiomatic manner, for example, 'always speaking softly to' or 'not raising one's voice.'[44]

When I come to the Messiah as someone who misses God's goal (aka sinner), I must come in humility. I acknowledge that I am a pauper and beggar who comes with nothing to offer Him but my heart and my need for salvation. I recognize my lack of merit and my complete inability to save myself.

---

[44] Louw, J. P., & Nida, E. A. (1996). *Greek-English lexicon of the New Testament: based on semantic domains* (electronic ed. of the second edition., Vol. 1, p. 748). New York: United Bible Societies.

Jesus offers the grace and mercy of God. We accept it in humble gratitude and commit our lives to Him and to our co-workers. We "die to self" so that we can live as new creations in the Messiah.

We never forget that He has exchanged our worthlessness for His infinite worth, our sin for His righteousness, and the life we now live, we live by faith in the Son of God who loved us and gave Himself for us. Now that is some exceptionally good news.

The "Jesus Way" goal for our faith at work: Jesus calls on us to meek and humble at work. It is the way to love. Jesus knows this and challenges us become organized. It is essential to bring glory to the name of Jesus.

Online Version: Can we be meek and humble at work? | Digital Business (wordpress.com)

7.6.2 What does Jesus teach about humility at work?

__That Jesus died for us is true humility.__ I must humble myself. I must cry out to Jesus to have mercy on me a sinner. I must remember who I am and where I came from. There is no such thing as servant leadership if the country where Jesus is King. Jesus is the leader. Jesus is the King. I am not.

__The "Jesus Way" goal for our faith at work:__ Jesus challenges us to be servants and slaves. Our job is to love and serve. That is, it. There is nothing else.

- Mark 9:33–37 —They came to Capernaum; and when He was in the house, He began to question them, "What were you discussing on the way?" But they kept silent, for on the way they had discussed with one another which of them was the greatest. Sitting down, He called the twelve and said to them, __"If anyone wants to be first, he shall be last of all and servant of all."__ Taking a child, He set him before them, and taking him in His arms, He said to them, "Whoever receives one child like this in My name receives Me; and whoever receives Me does not receive Me, but Him who sent Me."

- Matthew 23:8–12 — "But do not be called Rabbi; for One is your Teacher, and you are all brothers. Do not call anyone on earth your father; for One is your Father, He who is in heaven. Do not be called leaders; for One is your Leader, that is, the Messiah. But __the greatest among you shall be your servant__. __Whoever exalts himself shall be humbled; and whoever humbles himself shall be exalted.__"

- Mark 10:42–45 —Calling them to Himself, Jesus said to them, "You know that those who are recognized as rulers of the Gentiles Master it over them; and their great men exercise authority over them. But it is not this way among you, but __whoever wishes to become great among you shall be your servant__; and __whoever wishes to be first among you shall be slave of all__. For even the Son of Man did not come to be served, but to serve, and to give His life a ransom for many."

- Luke 14:7–11 —And He began speaking a parable to the invited guests when He noticed how they had been picking out the places of honor at the table, saying to them, "When you are invited by someone to a wedding feast, do not take the place of honor, for someone more distinguished than you may have been invited by him, and he who invited you both will come and say to you, 'Give your place to this man,' and then in disgrace you proceed to occupy the last place. "But when you are invited, go and recline at the last place, so that when the one who has invited you comes, he may say to you, 'Friend, move up higher'; then you will have honor in the sight of all who are at the table with you. "__For everyone who exalts himself will be humbled, and he who humbles himself will be exalted.__"

- Luke 18:9–14 —And He also told this parable to some people who trusted in themselves that they were righteous and viewed others with contempt: "Two men went up into the temple to pray, one a Pharisee and the other a tax collector. "The Pharisee stood and was praying this to himself: 'God, I thank You that I am not like other people: swindlers, unjust, adulterers, or even like this tax collector. 'I fast twice a week; I pay tithes of all that I get.' "But the tax collector, standing some distance away, was even unwilling to lift his eyes to heaven, but was beating his breast, saying, '**God, be merciful to me, the sinner**!' "I tell you; this man went to his house justified rather than the other; for **everyone who exalts himself will be humbled, but he who humbles himself will be exalted**."

Online Version: What does Jesus teach about humility at work? | Digital Business (wordpress.com)

7.6.3 What is humility at work?

Biblical humility is not only necessary to enter the kingdom, but also to be great in the kingdom.

> It must not be like that among you. On the contrary, **whoever wants to become great among you must be your servant, and whoever wants to be first among you must be your slave**.

(Matthew 20:26-27).

The "Jesus Way" goal for our faith at work: Jesus is our model. Just as He did not come to be served, but to serve, so must we commit ourselves to serving others, considering their interests above our own.

- Do nothing out of selfish ambition or conceit, but in humility consider others as more important than yourselves. (Philippians 2:3).
- This attitude precludes selfish ambition, conceit, and the strife that comes with self-justification and self-defense. Jesus was not ashamed to humble Himself as a servant Example washing the feet of the disciples (John 13:1-16),
- even to death on the cross he humbled himself by becoming obedient to the point of death—even to death on a cross. (Philippians 2:8).
- This attitude precludes selfish ambition, conceit, and the strife that comes with self-justification and self-defense. Jesus was not ashamed to humble Himself as a servant Example washing the feet of the disciples (John 13:1-16),
- even to death on the cross he humbled himself by becoming obedient to the point of death—even to death on a cross. (Philippians 2:8).

In His humility, He was always obedient to the Father and so should the humble disciple of Jesus be willing to put aside all selfishness and submit in obedience to God and His Word. True humility produces godliness, contentment, and security.

- God has promised to give grace to the humble, while He opposes the proud, He mocks those who mock but gives grace to the humble. (Proverbs 3:34).
- In the same way, you who are younger, be subject to the elders. All of you clothe yourselves with humility toward one another because God resists the proud but gives grace to the humble. (1 Peter 5:5).

Therefore, we must confess and put away pride. If we exalt ourselves, we place ourselves in opposition to God who will, in His grace and for our own good, humble us. But if we humble ourselves, God gives us more grace and exalts us.

> For **everyone who exalts himself will be humbled**, and the one who humbles himself will be exalted."

Along with Jesus, Paul is also to be our example of humility. Despite the great gifts and understanding he had received; Paul saw himself as the "least of the apostles" and the "chief of sinners."

- 15 This saying is trustworthy and deserving of full acceptance: "The Messiah Jesus came into the world to save sinners"—and I am the worst of them. (1 Timothy 1:15.
- 9 For I am the least of the apostles, not worthy to be called an apostle, because I persecuted the church of God.1 Corinthians 15:9).

Like Paul, the truly humble will glory in the grace of God and in the cross, not in self-righteousness.

- 3 For we are the circumcision, the ones who worship by the Spirit of God, boast in The Messiah Jesus, and do not put confidence in the flesh— 4 although I have reasons for confidence in the flesh. If anyone else thinks he has grounds for confidence in the flesh, I have more: 5 circumcised the eighth day; of the nation of Israel, of the tribe of Benjamin, a Hebrew born of Hebrews; regarding the law, a Pharisee; 6 regarding zeal, persecuting the church; regarding the righteousness that is in the law, blameless. (Philippians 3:3-7)

- 7 But everything that was a gain to me, I have considered to be a loss because of The Messiah. 8 More than that, I also consider everything to be a loss in view of the surpassing value of knowing The Messiah Jesus my Lord. Because of him I have suffered the loss of all things and consider them as dung, so that I may gain The Messiah 9 and be found in him, not having a righteousness of my own from the law, but one that is through faith in The Messiah—the righteousness from God based on faith. (Philippians 3:3-9).

Online Version: What is humility at work? | Digital Business (wordpress.com)

place it where it should be—on God and on helping others. As a disciple of Jesus, life is devoid of ego, the "I will" becomes a "thy will."

Online Version: What does the Bible say about our ego at work? | Digital Business (wordpress.com)

7.6.5 Jesus amazing example of humility for us at work.

Jesus washing the feet of the disciples (John 13:1–17) occurred in the upper room, during the Last Supper and has significance in three ways. For Jesus, it was the display of His humility and His servanthood. For the disciples, the washing of their feet was in direct contrast to their heart attitudes at that time. For us, washing feet is symbolic of our role in the body of the Messiah.

Walking in sandals on the filthy roads of Israel in the first century made it imperative that feet be washed before a communal meal, especially since people reclined at a low table and feet were very prominent. When Jesus rose from the table and began to wash the feet of the disciples (John 13:4), He was doing the work of the lowliest of servants. The disciples must have been stunned at this act of humility and condescension, that the Messiah, their Master, and master, should wash the feet of His disciples, when it was their proper work to have washed His. But when Jesus came to earth the first time, He came not as King and Conqueror, but as the suffering Servant of Isaiah 53. As He revealed in Matthew 20:28, He came "not to be served but to serve, and to give his life as a ransom for many." The humility expressed by His act with towel and basin foreshadowed His ultimate act of humility and love on the cross.

Jesus' attitude of servanthood was in direct contrast to that of the disciples, who had recently been arguing among themselves as to which of them was the greatest (Luke 22:24). Since there was no servant present to wash their feet, it would never have occurred to them to wash one another's feet. When the Master Himself stooped to this lowly task, they were stunned into silence. To his credit, though, Peter was profoundly uncomfortable with the Master washing his feet, and never being at a loss for words, Peter protested, "You shall never wash my feet!"

Then Jesus said something that must have further shocked Peter: "Unless I wash you, you have no part with me" (John 13:8), prompting Peter, whose love for the Savior was genuine, to request a complete washing. Then Jesus explained the true meaning of being washed by Him. Peter had experienced the cleansing of salvation and did not need to be washed again in the spiritual sense. Salvation is a one-time act of justification by faith, but the lifelong process of sanctification is one of washing from the stain of sin we experience as we walk through the world. Peter and the disciples—all except Judas, who never belonged to the Messiah—needed only this temporal cleansing.

This truth is just one of several from this incident that the disciples can apply to their own lives at work. First, when we come to the Messiah for the washing of our sins, we can be sure that is permanent and complete. No act can cleanse us further from our sin, as our sin has been exchanged for the perfect righteousness of the Messiah on the cross. But we do need continual cleansing of the effects of living in the flesh in a sin-cursed world. The continual washing of sanctification is done by the power of the Holy Spirit, who lives within us, through the "washing of water by the Word" (Ephesians 5:26), given to us to equip us for every clever work (2 Timothy 3:16–17).

Further, when Jesus washed the disciples' feet, He told them (and us), "I have given you an example, that you should do as I have done to you" (John 13:15). As His followers, we are to emulate Him, serving one another in lowliness of heart and mind, looking to build one another up in humility and love. When we seek preeminence, we displease the Master who promised that true greatness in His kingdom is reached by those with a servant's heart. When we have that servant's heart, the Master promised, we will be blessed.

The "Jesus Way" goal for our faith at work: This is straightforward. We learn humility by following the example of Jesus.

Online Version: Jesus amazing example of humility for us at work. | Digital Business (wordpress.com)

7.6.6 Why is humility at work important to Jesus?

Why it matters: Nobody really likes egotistical and arrogant people. It is not the way of love. It is not the way of Jesus. We must take the initiative to humble ourselves. We must take the initiative to focus on serving others at work.

> And He also told this parable to some people who trusted in themselves that they were righteous and viewed others with contempt: "Two men went up into the temple to pray, one a Pharisee and the other a tax collector. "The Pharisee stood and was praying this to himself: 'God, I thank You that I am not like other people: swindlers, unjust, adulterers, or even like this tax collector. 'I fast twice a week; I pay tithes of all that I get.' "But the tax collector, standing some distance away, was even unwilling to lift his eyes to heaven, but was beating his breast, saying, **'God, be merciful to me, the sinner**!' "I tell you; this man went to his house justified rather than the other; for **everyone who exalts himself will be humbled, but he who humbles himself will be exalted**."

Luke 18:9–14

Some questions to consider:

- What is the result, according to Jesus, if we are humble at work?

- Why does that result become important for God's message at work?

- What are the things we should boast about at work?

- What implications are there for us with our colleagues in the example of Jesus washing the feet of the disciples?

The way I see it: Jesus emphasizes our role. Our role is to humble ourselves and not wait for others (or God) to do it for us. It is our choice. We get to decide. What will it be?

Good news: Jesus has given us a gift. That gift is our advocate, the Holy Spirit, the power to live a sanctified and humble life.

Online Version: Why is humility at work important to Jesus? | Digital Business (wordpress.com)

- **My words at work will be judged.** Note the words spoken to the two visitors in James 2:3. What we say to people, and how we say it, will come up before God. Even our careless words will be judged (Matt. 12:36). Of course, the words we speak come from the heart; so, when God judges the words, He is examining the heart (Matt. 12:34–37). Jesus emphasized caution when speaking in some of His warnings in the Sermon on the Mount (Matt. 5:21–26, 33–37; 7:1–5, 21–23).
- **My deeds at work will be judged.** Read Colossians 3:22–25 for more insight. It is true that God remembers our sins against us no more (Jer. 31:34; Heb. 10:17); but our sins affect our character and works. We cannot sin lightly and serve faithfully. God forgives our sins when we confess them to Him, but He will not change their consequences.
- **My attitude at work will be judged** James contrasted two attitudes: showing mercy to others and refusing to show mercy. If we have been merciful toward others, God can be merciful toward us. However, we must not twist this truth into a lie.

It does not mean that we earn mercy by showing mercy, because it is impossible to earn mercy. If it is earned, it is not mercy! Nor does it mean that we should "be soft on sin" and never judge it in the lives of others. "I don't condemn anybody," a man once told me, "and God won't condemn me." How wrong he was!

Mercy and justice both come from God, so they are not competitors. Where God finds repentance and faith, He can show mercy; where He finds rebellion and unbelief, He must administer justice. It is the heart of the sinner that decides the treatment he gets. Our Lord's parable in Matthew 18:21–35 illustrates the truth. The parable is not illustrating salvation, but forgiveness between fellow servants. If we forgive our brothers, then we have the kind of heart that is open toward the forgiveness of God.

We shall be judged "by the Law of liberty." Why does James use this title for God's Law? For one thing, when we obey God's Law, it frees us from sin and enables us to walk in liberty (Ps. 119:45). Also, law prepares us for liberty. A child must be under rules and regulations because he is not mature enough to handle the decisions and demands of life. He is given outward discipline so that he might develop inward discipline, and one day be free of rules.

Liberty does not mean license. License (doing whatever I want to do) is the worst kind of bondage. Liberty means the freedom to be all that I can be in Jesus the Messiah. License is confinement; liberty is fulfillment.

Finally, the Word is called "the Law of liberty" because God sees our hearts and knows what we would have done had we been free to do so. The student who obeys only because the school has rules is not really maturing.

What will I do when I leave school? God's Word can change my heart and give me the desire to do God's will, so that I obey from inward compulsion and not outward constraint.

There is one obvious message to this section: our beliefs should control our behavior. If we really believe that Jesus is the Son of God, and that God is gracious, His Word is true, and one day He will judge us, then our conduct will reveal our convictions. Before we attack those, who do not have orthodox doctrine, we must be sure that we practice the doctrines we defend. Jonah had wonderful theology, but he hated people and was angry with God (Jonah 4).

One of the tests of the reality of our faith at work is how I treat other people. Can I pass the test?

The "Jesus Way" goal for our faith at work: We are to lead the way in showing mercy and being kind to our co-workers. We should never wait on others. This requires us to love unconditionally.

Some questions to consider:

- A colleague makes a big mistake. Will we advocate for their dismissal or for them to be given another opportunity and to learn from their mistake?
- Will we suspend our judgement of others and search for the facts first?
- Will we mention Jesus as the standard for how we treat others?

Online Version: A leader's role in mercy and kindness. | Digital Business (wordpress.com)

7.9 HOW DOES BEING <u>PURE IN HEART</u> MAKE A DIFFERENCE AT OUR WORKPLACE?

> *<u>Blessed [fortunate] are the pure in heart, for they will see God</u>.* [48]
>
> ~Jesus (Matthew 5:8)

Our motives, at work, make a difference. Motives are a matter of the heart. Jesus challenges us to make sure, in workplaces, that our heart is pure.

In the sixth principle in the Jesus Manifesto (Matthew 5-7), Jesus goes to the core of human life, the heart. Purity or cleanliness was an important religious theme in Jesus' day. Jesus declares here that a pure heart in our work, is what produces external purity, not vice versa. Our colleagues will see it.

While the people of the bible knew clearly that the human heart was critical, they knew equally well that God's work in an evil heart could bring purification and a new motivation for following him.

- "Create in me a pure heart, O God, and renew a steadfast spirit in me" (Ps. 51:10).
- The pure in heart are those who have not follow all the rules at work but who nonetheless have given undivided loyalty to God and his ways.

The undivided devotion of the pure in heart will be rewarded by their greatest hope: "They will see God." While no human can look fully at the glorious face of God, the hope that culminates this age is that "they will see his face, and his name will be on their foreheads" (Rev. 22:4). But Jesus' pronouncement of this principle to those of his day also has an immediate fulfillment of their hopes. Jesus is Immanuel, "God with us" (Luke 1:23).

The "Jesus Way" goal for our faith at work: We must set our heart on God at work. We must not simply follow corporate ritualism. We must respond to Jesus' message of the good news of the Jesus reign at work. We will be invited to enter a fellowship with him in which they will experience the unthinkable; we will see God in Jesus. And at work, they will see Jesus in us.

Some questions to consider:

- Are we committed to being pure in our hearts at work?

---

[48] *New American Standard Bible*. (2020). (Mt 5:8). La Habra, CA: The Lockman Foundation.

- ✓ God is Holy – God is Infinitely, Unchangingly Perfect
- ✓ God Is Glorious – He is Infinitely Beautiful and Great

Why this is important: God is God. God wants us to keep "the big picture" in mind as we work out our faith at work.

Online Version: Because of our purity of heart at work, we are going to see God. Who is God? | Digital Business (wordpress.com)

7.9.5 What is it for us to be pure in heart at work?

The "Jesus Way" goal for our faith at work: God desires for us a level of purity of heart at work that always brings glory to Him, His Son Jesus, and the Holy Spirit.

- Are we bringing Him glory with our focus on purity?
- Are we standing for the truth of Jesus and what is not deceitful?

Søren Kierkegaard authored a book called *Purity of Heart Is to Will One Thing*. That is not a bad definition, provided that the one thing we will is the glory of God at work.

According To David Let me try to show you where that definition comes from in Scripture. We start with the closest OT parallel to this beatitude, namely, Psalm 24:3–4:

> *Who shall ascend the hill of Yahweh?*
> *And who shall stand in his holy place?*
> *He who has clean hands and a pure heart,*
> *who does not lift his soul to what is false,*
> *and does not swear deceitfully.*

You can see what David means by a "pure heart" at work in the phrases that follow it.

- A pure heart is a heart that has nothing to do with falsehood.
- It is painstakingly truthful and free from deceitfulness.
- Deceit is what you do when you will two things, not one thing.
- You will to do one thing and you will that people think you are doing another. You will to feel one thing and you will that people think you are feeling another.
- That is impurity of heart. Purity of heart is to will one thing, namely, to "seek the face of Yahweh" (verse 6).

According to James You can see this idea of purity in our work in James 4:8:

> *Draw near to God and he will draw near to you. Cleanse your hands,*
> *you sinners, and purify your hearts, you men of double mind.*

Notice that just like Psalm 24 there is reference to both clean hands and a pure heart as preparation for drawing near to God, or "ascending the hill of the Master." But notice how the men are described who need to purify their hearts: "men of double mind." That is, they are men that will two things not just one thing. The impurity of doublemindedness is explained in James 4:4-10:

> **You adulterous people! Do you not know that friendship with the world is enmity with God?** Therefore, whoever wishes to be a friend of the world makes himself an enemy of God. [5] Or do you suppose it

> is to no purpose that the Scripture says, "He yearns jealously over the spirit that he has made to dwell in us"? **6** But he gives more grace. Therefore, it says, "God opposes the proud but gives grace to the humble." **7** Submit yourselves therefore to God. Resist the devil, and he will flee from you. **8** Draw near to God, and he will draw near to you. <u>**Cleanse your hands, you sinners, and purify your hearts, you double-minded.**</u> **9** Be wretched and mourn and weep. Let your laughter be turned to mourning and your joy to gloom. **10** Humble yourselves before the Lord, and he will exalt you. [50]

So, the double-minded man of verse 8 has his heart divided between the world and God, like a wife who has a husband and a boyfriend. Purity of heart at work, on the other hand, is to will one thing, namely, full, and total allegiance to God.

From Jesus's Mouth: So, if we ask, Where in the gospels did Jesus explain purity of heart in this way? The answer would be Matthew 22:37:

> *You shall love the Master your God with all your heart.*

Not with part of your heart. Not with a double or divided heart. That would be impurity. The purity of the heart is no deception, no doublemindedness, no divided allegiance.

"God is the one who purifies the heart, and the instrument with which he cleans it is faith."

You can see the echo of this meaning of purity of heart in 1 Timothy 1:5,

> <u>**"The aim of our charge is loving those issues from a pure heart and a good conscience and sincere [i.e., unhypocritical faith].**</u>"

Purity of heart at work is to will one thing, namely, God's truth and God's value in everything we do. The aim of the pure heart is to align itself with the truth of God and magnify the worth of God. If you want to be pure in heart, pursue God with utter single-mindedness. Purity of heart is to will that one thing.

Online Version: What is it for us to be pure in heart at work? | Digital Business (wordpress.com)

---

[50] *The Holy Bible: English Standard Version* (Wheaton, IL: Crossway Bibles, 2016), Jas 4:4–10.

7.9.6 How do the pure in heart at work see God?

> ***Blessed [fortunate] are the pure in heart, for they will see God.*** [51]
>
> ~Jesus (Matthew 5:8)

Jesus only gives us part of the answer here. It is a true part, but only part. He says that the pure at work will see God. That is, purity is a prerequisite for seeing God. The impure are neither granted admittance to his presence, nor are they awed by the glory of his holiness, nor are they comforted by his grace.

Jesus's point is the same as Hebrews 12:14: "Strive for . . . the holiness without which no one will see the Master." In other words, blessed are the holy for they shall see God. There is a real purity and a real holiness which suits us to see the king of glory.

And of course, that leads every sensitive soul at work to cry out with the words of Proverbs 20:9, "Who can say, 'I have made my heart clean; I am pure from my sin?'" And with the disciples: "Who then can be saved?"

Jesus's answer comes back just like it did to the disciples in Matthew 19:26 — and this is the rest of the answer — "With men it is impossible, but with God all things are possible." In other words, God creates a purity for us and in us so that we can pursue purity. And by his grace we must seek that gift by praying with David, "Create in me a clean heart, O God" (Psalm 51:10). And we must look to the Messiah "who gave himself for us . . . to purify for himself a people" (Titus 2:14).

And the response of our hearts to God's act of creation and the Messiah's act of sacrifice is single-minded faith in Jesus the Messiah as Master of our life at work and Savior. As the Scripture says in Acts 15:9, "God made no distinction between us and them, but purified their hearts by faith."

God is the one who purifies the heart, and the instrument with which he cleans it is faith. "Therefore, trust in the Master with *all* your heart" (Proverbs 3:5). Will this one thing. And you will see God.

Jesus Himself testifies that His word purifies us. It has already happened. It is a fact.

- **John 15:3 — "You are already clean because of the word which I have spoken to you."**

---

[51] *New American Standard Bible*. (2020). (Mt 5:8). La Habra, CA: The Lockman Foundation.

- **John 13:10** —Jesus said to him, "He who has bathed needs only to wash his feet, but is completely clean; and **you are clean**, but not all of you."

It is our job to focus on seeing God and resisting temptation.

- **James 4:7–8** —Submit therefore to God. **Resist the devil and he will flee from you.** 8 Draw near to God and He will draw near to you. Cleanse your hands, you sinners; and purify your hearts, you double-minded.

- **1 Peter 5:9** —But **resist him, firm in your faith,** knowing that the same experiences of suffering are being carried out by your brethren who are in the world.

It is up to us to deny worldly desires. It is up to us to purify ourselves.

- **Titus 2:12–13** —instructing us **to deny ungodliness and worldly desires and to live sensibly, righteously, and godly in the present age**, looking for the blessed hope and the appearing of the glory of our great God and Savior, the Messiah Jesus,

- **1 John 3:3** —And **everyone who has this hope fixed on Him purifies himself**, just as He is pure.

Online Version: How do the pure in heart at work see God? | Jesus Quotes and God Thoughts (wordpress.com)

7.10 ARE WE KNOWN FOR BEING PEACEMAKERS IN THE WORKPLACE?

__Blessed [fortunate] are the peacemakers, for they will be called sons of God.__ [52]

~Jesus (Matthew 5:9)

The seventh principle of the start of the Jesus Manifesto focuses on "the peacemakers" at work. The theme of "peace" permeates the biblical record. It shows completeness and wholeness in every area of life, including one's relationship with colleagues and employees at work.

Jesus turns aside the various political, religious, and corporate attempts of those within our workplaces to set up their supremacy. They have created even more division; thus, he turns to those who want God's peace. With the inauguration of the kingdom of heaven, Jesus himself is the supreme peacemaker, making peace between God and humans, and among humans, particularly at work. Those who have waited for God's messianic peace can now respond to Jesus' invitation, and they will receive the ultimate reward: to be called "sons of God," fulfilling the role that Israel has assumed but taken for granted. Those who respond to Jesus' ministry are heirs of the kingdom and reflect the character of their heavenly Father as they carry Jesus' mission of peacemaking to the corporate world.

Every follower of Jesus, according to this happiness prescription, is meant to be a peacemaker at work and in the church. True, Jesus was to say later that he had 'not come to bring peace, but a sword', for he had come 'to set a man against his father, and a daughter against her mother, and a daughter-in-law against her mother-in-law', so that a man's enemies would be 'those of his own household' and at your place of work.

God's goal: What he meant by this was that conflict would be the inevitable result of his coming, even in one's own colleagues, and that, if we are to be worthy of him, we must love him best and put him first, above even our nearest and dearest co-workers. It is clear beyond question throughout the teaching of Jesus and his apostles that we should never ourselves seek conflict or handle it.

On the contrary, we are called to peace, we are actively to 'pursue' peace, we are to 'strive for peace with all men,' and so far, as it depends on us, we are to 'live peaceably with all.'

---

[52] *New American Standard Bible*. (2020). (Mt 5:9). La Habra, CA: The Lockman Foundation.

7.10.3   The importance of pursuing peace at work

Blessed [fortunate] are the peacemakers, for they will be called sons of God. [53]

~Jesus (Matthew 5:9)

It is hardly surprising that the benefit which attaches to peacemakers at work is that 'they shall be called sons of God.' For they are looking to do what their Father has done, loving people with his love, as Jesus is soon to make explicit. It is the devil who is a troublemaker; it is God who loves reconciliation and who now through his children, as formerly through his only begotten Son, is bent on making peace.

The importance of pursuing peace at work: I cannot make peace if I do not have peace myself. That is the first task, find peace in Jesus. Then, I can make peace by proclaiming His word and carrying on with His deeds in the corporate world.

- Ecclesiastes 10:4 — If the ruler's temper rises against you, **do not abandon your position**, because composure allays great offenses.
- Romans 12:18 — If possible, as far as it depends on you, **be at peace with all men**.
- Titus 1:6 — namely, if any man is above reproach, the husband of one wife, having children who believe, **not accused of dissipation or rebellion**.
- Hebrews 12:14 — **Pursue peace with all men**, and the sanctification without which no one will see the Master.
- James 3:17 — **But the wisdom from above is first pure, then peaceable**, gentle, reasonable, full of mercy and good fruits, unwavering, without hypocrisy.

Jesus prayed for the oneness of his people. He also prayed that they might be kept from evil and in truth. We have no mandate from the Messiah to seek unity without purity, purity of both belief and conduct. If there is such a thing as 'cheap reunion,' there is 'cheap evangelism' also, namely the proclamation of the good news without the cost of discipleship, the demand for faith without repentance. These are forbidden short cuts. They turn the messenger of good news into a fraud. They cheapen the good news of Jesus and damage the cause of the Messiah.

Peace at work in a believer's relationship with Jesus There are times I am clearly not at peace. I am not at peace with myself, and I am not at peace with God or Jesus. Something is wrong. I may or may not know it, but it becomes clear in my anxiety and

---

[53] *New American Standard Bible*. (2020). (Mt 5:9). La Habra, CA: The Lockman Foundation.

worry. I am <u>not convinced</u>, at that point in time, that God is good and has my best interest at heart.

It starts with faith. I need to get clear with my faith in Jesus. When peace leaves me, I need to get back to the real issue. I do not have faith; I do not believe who Jesus is and what He carried out. Lack of peace comes from ignoring the core issue of unbelief. God is good. God sent His son to make me right with God. God did it out of love for me. Now that is some good news!

> *"Therefore, having been justified by faith, we have peace with God through our Master Jesus the Messiah."*

Romans 5:1

Online Version: <u>The importance of pursuing peace at work | Digital Business (wordpress.com)</u>

7.10.4 Reconciliation with Jesus sets up peace at work.

How often do I start condemning myself when my faith at work is faltering? Way too often. The enemy loves to get me down this way. I start believing a lie about God and Jesus. They love me because I am such a mess. It is a lie because by the love of God, I am a new person. I have died and been resurrected with Jesus. Again, good news and no condemnation.

> ***Therefore, there is now no condemnation for those who are in the Messiah Jesus.***

Romans 8:1

This is a stunning statement from the Apostle Paul. I need to come back to it repeatedly. Is God against me? Does Jesus condemn me? The answer is a resounding NO! Nothing can separate me from the love of God.

Peace in a believer's relationship with Jesus.

> *What then shall we say to these things? If God is for us, who is against us? He who did not spare His own Son, but delivered Him over for us all, how will He not also with Him freely give us all things? Who will bring a charge against God's elect? God is the one who justifies; who is the one who condemns? The Messiah Jesus is He who died, yes, who was raised, who is at the right hand of God, who also intercedes for us. Who will separate us from the love of the Messiah? Will tribulation, distress, persecution, famine, or nakedness, or peril, or sword? Just as it is written, "For Your sake we are being put to death all day long; We were considered as sheep to be slaughtered." But in all these things we overwhelmingly conquer through Him who loved us. **For I am convinced that neither death, nor life, nor angels, nor principalities, nor things present, nor things to come, nor powers, nor height, nor depth, nor any other created thing, will be able to separate us from the love of God, which is in the Messiah Jesus our Master.***

|Romans 8:31–39

And so … Peace is ours at work. That is the promise and that is the truth. It is a gift from our heavenly Father.

> *To the church of God which is at Corinth, to those who have been sanctified in the Messiah Jesus, saints by calling, with all who in every place call on the name of our Master Jesus the Messiah, their*

1 Corinthians 1:2–3

What does the teachings of Jesus tell us about peace at work? In Romans 12:18, Paul exhorts, "If possible, so far as it depends on you, be at peace with all men [co-workers]." What a perfect example of my role in the fruit of the Spirit mentioned in Galatians 5:22-23. I am to give my will to God's leading at work and my actions to God's Word, but the actual results are up to Him.

Only God can create peace through the work of the Holy Spirit. Especially the peace mentioned in Galatians 5—the peace of a harmonious relationship with God.

- Acts 10:36 — The word which He sent to the sons of Israel, **preaching peace through Jesus the Messiah** (He is Master of all).
- John 16:33 — "These things I have spoken to you, s<u>o that in Me you may have peace</u>. In the world you have tribulation but take courage; I have overcome the world."
- John 14:23–27 — Jesus answered and said to him, "If anyone loves Me, he will keep My word; and My Father will love him, and We will come to him and make Our abode with him. He who does not love Me does not keep My words; and the word which you hear is not Mine, but the Father's who sent Me. These things I have spoken to you while abiding with you. But the Helper, the Holy Spirit, whom the Father will send in My name, He will teach you all things, and bring to your remembrance all that I said to you. **Peace, I leave with you; My peace I give to you**; not as the world gives do I give to you. **Do not let your heart be troubled, nor let it be fearful**."
- John 15:3 — "**You are already clean** because of the word which I have spoken to you."

There is good news! We have peace with God through the blood that Jesus shed on the cross. We were estranged from God. We did not know Him and were separated from Him. We were an enemy of God. We need Jesus. Jesus brings peace and reconciliation at work.

How can a holy God ever be reconciled with sinful man? Can God lower His standards, close His eyes to sin, and compromise with man? If He did, the universe would fall to pieces! God must be consistent with Himself and keep His own holy Law.

Man could somehow please God. But by nature, man is separated from God; and by his deeds, he is alienated from God. The sinner is "dead in trespasses and sins," and therefore is unable to do anything to save himself or to please God.

Reconciliation with Jesus If there is to be reconciliation between man and God, the initiative and action must come from God. It is in the Messiah Jesus that God was reconciled to man. But it was not the incarnation of Jesus that carried out this reconciliation, nor was it His example as He lived among men. It was through His death that peace was made between God and man. He "made peace through the blood of His cross."

- Colossians 1:19–20 (NASB) —For it was the Father's good pleasure for all the fullness to dwell in Him, and through Him to reconcile all things to Himself, **having made peace through the blood of His cross**; through Him, I say, whether things on earth or things in heaven.
- Isaiah 53:5 —But He was pierced through for our transgressions, He was crushed for our iniquities; The chastening for our well-being fell upon Him, And **by His scourging we are healed**.

Jesus is our peace and brings unity with God.

- Matthew 26:26–28 —While they were eating, Jesus took some bread, and after a blessing, He broke it and gave it to the disciples, and said, "Take, eat; this is My body." And when He had taken a cup and given thanks, He gave it to them, saying, "Drink from it, all of you; for **this is My blood of the covenant, which is poured out for many for forgiveness of sins**.
- Galatians 6:14–16 —But may it never be that I would boast, except in the cross of our Master Jesus the Messiah, **through which the world has been crucified to me**, and I to the world. For neither is circumcision anything, nor uncircumcision, but a new creation. And **those who will walk by this rule, peace and mercy be upon them, and upon the Israel of God**.
- Ephesians 2:13–17 —But now in the Messiah Jesus you who formerly were far off have been brought near by the blood of the Messiah. **For He Himself is our peace, who made both groups into one and broke down the barrier of the dividing wall**, by abolishing in His flesh the enmity,

Application

- What does it mean to be a peacemaker?
- Why is being a peacemaker important?
- How can we improve our skills at peacemaking?
- What are some things we can do, at work, to be more of a peacemaker in the next 7 days?

Online Version: Reconciliation with Jesus sets up peace at work | Digital Business (wordpress.com)

7.11 ARE WE READY TO BE INSULTED AND PERSECUTED BY OUR COLLEAGUES AND BOSS?

> *Blessed [fortunate] are you when people [co-workers] insult you and persecute you, and falsely say all kinds of evil against you because of Me*. Rejoice and be glad, for your reward in heaven is great; for in this same way, they persecuted the prophets who were before you. [54]

~Jesus (Matthew 5:11-12)

The emphasis in the "Jesus Manifesto" shifts increasingly from *pronouncement* to the crowds and the corporate leadership to *instruction* for Jesus' disciples. This is important to us, in our life at work. Insults and lies about us hurt. The corporate leadership and our colleagues will insult, persecute, and utter evil against the disciples in God's name, but Jesus will reveal these leaders to be no different than the hypocritical leaders of the Old Testament, who persecuted God's true prophets.

- The harassment his disciples receive is more specific than "because of righteousness;" it is "because of me."
- Since Jesus himself will experience opposition and persecution, his disciples should expect the same.
- It will happen at work. Count on it and prepare for it.

In this instruction Jesus prepares his disciples for the time when persecution will indeed come to them, offering them the hope that no matter how hard the circumstances, they are truly heirs of the kingdom. It will come to us at work. Although the kingdom belongs to us, it does not currently usher in a time of peace and safety.

In fact, Jesus shows that their reward will not come in an earthly kingdom but "in heaven." He looks down the long corridor of time until the kingdom is set up on earth in its final form and offers hope during those times when it seems doubtful that his kingdom will ever arrive. It may not look like it from a religious, corporate, or social perspective, but the kingdom is ours nonetheless—and in this we will truly rejoice.

How should we act when we are insulted at work? The way of Jesus is the Way of Love. Later in the manifesto (Matthew 5-7), Jesus shows us we must love our enemies. We can prepare now by loving now. We can also prepare by playing a few likely scenarios out and ask God for wisdom on how to act.

---

[54] *New American Standard Bible*. (2020). (Mt 5:10–12). La Habra, CA: The Lockman Foundation.

We should expect to be persecuted at work. Jesus said it. It is normal for a disciple. Why? Because following Jesus and living in His righteousness threatens so many. Want to find out how threatening it is? Proclaim the truth to the "new atheists" and see what happens. Live in a socialist or communist country and follow Jesus.

We have gotten comfortable in the U. S. It is coming.

The principles laid out here by Jesus in his manifesto are not entrance requirements to the kingdom of God, or else Jesus would be sanctioning torture or martyrdom as a way of earning one's entrance to the kingdom. At the same time, this again makes clear that they are not ethical demands for personal behavior at work, or else Jesus would be implying that it would be good for his disciples to seek out persecution to gain his blessing.

Jesus comforts those who have suffered undeserved persecution at work. Persecution for one's own sin or foolishness may be deserved, but these people have been persecuted because of their stand for righteousness.

- Persecution at work may come in many forms.
- We can be disciplined for speaking up.
- We might get fired. It happens at work with increasing frequency.
- Are we ready? Fear of it will paralyze our witness to the good news of Jesus.

Persecution can take the form of physical or verbal abuse, or both, but it especially points to the way that the religious leaders hounded the populace and excluded from their fellowship any who did not meet up to their standards. Exclusion from the right groups at work is immensely powerful. Corporate leaders should seek out the righteous at work. Forces are at work that led them in other directions.

As difficult as is the persecution, the reward far outweighs the hazard, because "ours is the kingdom of heaven." This is a present tense declaration. Jesus here gives hope to the people of his day who have stood up and contended for God's form of righteousness against the self-righteousness of the corporate leaders. Although we will be persecuted for it, Jesus says that the kingdom of God belongs to us, not the corporate leaders, and all they need to do now is to respond to his invitation to join the kingdom.[55]

God's people have always faced persecution in their jobs. The prophets were reviled, tortured, and killed. History records that ten of Jesus' disciples were executed for preaching the Messiah. Tradition states that Peter insisted on being crucified upside down because he counted himself unworthy to die in the same manner as his Master. Yet he wrote,

---

[55] Wilkins, M. J. (2004). *Matthew* (pp. 210–211). Grand Rapids, MI: Zondervan Publishing House.

> *"If you are reviled for the name of the Messiah, you are blessed, because the Spirit of God and of glory rests on you."*

(1 Peter 4:14).

The apostle Paul was jailed, beaten, shipwrecked, and stoned many times for preaching the Messiah, but he considered suffering not even worth mentioning compared to the reward he knew awaited in paradise.

- 2 Timothy 3:12 —Indeed**, all who desire to live godly in the Messiah Jesus [at work] will be persecuted**.
- Matthew 13:21 —Yet he has no firm root in himself, but is only temporary, and when affliction or **persecution arises because of the word**, at once he falls away.
- Mark 10:29–30 —Jesus said, "Truly I say to you, there is no one who has left house or brothers or sisters or mother or father or children or farms, for My sake and for the sake of the good news, but that he will receive a hundred times as much now in the present age, houses and brothers and sisters and mothers and children and farms, **along with persecutions**; and in the age to come, eternal life.
- 1 Thessalonians 3:4 —For indeed when we were with you, **we kept telling you in advance that we were going to suffer affliction**; and so, it happened, as you know.

Here are some issues that could be a challenge. Are you ready?

- Abortion – What happens when your CEO becomes a member of the local Planned Parenthood chapter and encourages others to get involved and donate?
- LGBT issues – What will happen when you refuse to use pronouns other than those corresponding only the two genders of male and female?
- CRT – What will happen when you refuse to admit you are a racist?
- Freedom of Religion – What will you do when you are asked not to wear your cross or take down the scripture you have posted at your desk? What will you do when you are asked not to talk about Jesus?

Online Version: Are we ready to be insulted by our colleagues and boss? | Digital Business (wordpress.com)

7.12 WE ARE TO BE THE SALT OF THE WORKPLACE.

> **You are the salt of the earth**; but if the salt has become tasteless,
> how can it be made salty again? It is no longer good for anything,
> except to be thrown out and trampled underfoot by people. [56]

~Jesus (Matthew 5:13)

Jesus is citing a known proverbial saying on impossibilities to describe an equally impossible characteristic of his disciples and our value at work. As we go out into the corporate world as salt, we must recognize that the proof of the reality of our profession is our lives. Do our colleagues see us as a necessary seasoning to our work mission? Do they seek us out because of the value we add?

- True disciples cannot lose what has made them disciples, because they have become changed persons, made new by the life of the kingdom of heaven bring faith in Jesus to the workplace.
- However, imposter disciples, who simply try to put on the flavoring of the kingdom life, will be revealed in the fire of the corporate environment.
- Their salt is only an external flavoring, not a personal change. Others, at work, will see it.
- This imposter cannot be made salty again because he or she never had that kingdom life in the first place.

Jesus' next statement drives home the seriousness of the issue at work: "It is no longer good for anything, except to be thrown out and trampled by men." The response to imposter disciples is rejection and judgment by co-workers for whom they are to have value. Imposters will be known for what they are.

- They have nothing to offer the corporate world because they are no different from their co-workers.
- So, the world turns on them for their arrogant hypocrisy.
- The challenge is for professing disciples to examine their nature and to confess honestly whether they have been transformed by the life of the kingdom of God.
- If not, we have lost our value to Jesus in the corporate marketplace.

---

[56] *New American Standard Bible*. (2020). (Mt 5:13). La Habra, CA: The Lockman Foundation.

Source: Wilkins, M. J. (2004). Matthew (p. 214). Grand Rapids, MI: Zondervan Publishing House.

Online Version: <u>Are we to be the salt of the workplace? | Digital Business</u> <u>(wordpress.com)</u>

7.13 WE ARE TO BE THE LIGHT OF THE WORKPLACE.

> ***You are the light of the world.*** *A city set on a hill cannot be hidden;* [15] *nor do people light a lamp and put it under a basket, but on the lampstand, it gives light to all who are in the house.* [16] *Your light must shine before people in such a way that they may see your good works and glorify your Father who is in heaven.* [57]

~Jesus (Matthew 5:14-16)

Jesus' disciples in the workplace are not only "the salt of the earth" but also "the light of the world." The light metaphor continues the salt metaphor and takes it one step further to illustrate Jesus' point of our faith at work. "Light" is an important theme in Scripture, normally emphasizing the removal of darkness in the unfolding of biblical history and theology.

This is enormously powerful for how we work out our faith at work. The literal contrast between physical light and darkness provokes a profound metaphorical contrast between metaphysical good and evil. Jesus later declares that he is "the light of the world," who has come as the light that enlightens all our co-workers, so that those believing in him will no longer be in darkness.

Jesus continues the proverbial "impossible" language he used in the salt metaphor by saying that "a city on a hill cannot be hidden," and "neither do people light a lamp and put it under a bowl." We are to be a light to the world which means we are to be a light at work. Our faith should drive out the darkness of sin at work.

Jesus' disciples are called to be the light of the workplace. They cannot be hidden, for their very nature, the kingdom life within them, is living testimony to those co-workers in the workplace who do not yet have that light.

- Their good works are produced by the light and life that come from God.
- It is not of their own making, because those who see them in action will glorify not them but their "Father in heaven."
- The title "Father" is used in Matthew here for the first time, introducing the special relationship that exists between God and Jesus' disciples.

---

[57] *New American Standard Bible*. (2020). (Mt 5:14–16). La Habra, CA: The Lockman Foundation.

Jesus' disciples have kingdom life at work, which produces honorable deeds from a changed life. Bearing the light of the good news in both message and life will bring people to know that the kingdom of heaven truly is in the place of work, and they will glorify their heavenly Father. The Jesus Manifesto principles hinted at this direction, but the metaphors of salt and light are the first explicit sign that the presence of the kingdom produces changed lives.

Source: Wilkins, M. J. (2004). Matthew (pp. 214–216). Grand Rapids, MI: Zondervan Publishing House.

Online Version: We are to be the light of the workplace. | Digital Business (wordpress.com)

7.14 How important is the righteousness of our lives at work?

> Do not presume that I came to abolish the Law or the Prophets; I did not come to abolish, but to fulfill. For truly I say to you, until heaven and earth pass away, not the smallest letter or stroke of a letter shall pass from the Law, until all is carried out! Therefore, whoever nullifies one of the least of these commandments, and teaches others to do the same, shall be called least in the kingdom of heaven; but whoever keeps and teaches them, he shall be called great in the kingdom of heaven.
>
> "For I say to you that **unless your righteousness far surpasses that of the scribes and Pharisees, you will not enter the kingdom of heaven.** [58]

~Jesus (Matthew 5:17-20)

At work, we have lots of rules and regulations. If our company has been around long enough, we have volumes of them. Our leaders at work are rule makers, rule enforcers and rule followers. They want to see us comply. Sometimes, however, they do not follow the rules they have made up. Everyone knows it and abhors that type of behavior of leaders.

Jesus has given us a roadmap to navigate it all. Mercy, for example, will triumph over 100 pages of HR policies. Jesus challenges us, in our faith at work, to live on a higher level than the elite rule makers and their enforcement arms.

What is righteousness in the context of our work environment? We can start with this definition from Wayne Grudem:

> *Righteousness means that God always acts following what is right and is himself the final standard of what is right.*[59]

---

[58] *New American Standard Bible*. (2020). (Matthew 5:17–20). La Habra, CA: The Lockman Foundation.

[59] Grudem, W. (2020). *Systematic Theology: An Introduction to Biblical Doctrine* (Second Edition, p. 243). Grand Rapids, MI: Zondervan Academic.

When we hear Jesus' talk about our righteousness, it means we act in accordance what is right from God's perspective. We must be at a higher level than the HR policy details. Our job at work is to reflect the righteousness of God. How will we exceed the righteousness of our corporate elites? Here are some starting points from Jesus.

- Be **poor in spirit.**
- **Mourn**
- Be **humble.**
- **Hunger and thirst for righteousness**
- Be **merciful**.
- Focus on being **pure in heart.**
- Be a **peacemaker.**

That should be enough for our day at work!

Online Version: How important is the righteousness of our lives at work? | Digital Business (wordpress.com)

7.15 Is anger at work dangerous for us?

> "You have heard that the ancients were told, 'You shall not murder,' and 'Whoever commits murder shall be answerable to the court.' **²² But I say to you that everyone who is angry with his brother shall be answerable to the court**; and whoever says to his brother, 'You good-for-nothing,' shall be answerable to ᵗhe supreme court; and whoever says, 'You fool,' shall be guilty enough to go into the ᶠiery hell. ²³ Therefore, if you are presenting your offering at the altar, and there you remember that your brother has something against you, ²⁴ leave your offering there before the altar and go; first be reconciled to your brother, and then come and present your offering. ²⁵ ¹Come to good terms with your accuser quickly, while you are with him on the way to court, so that your accuser will not hand you over to the judge, and the judge to the officer, and you will not be thrown into prison. ²⁶ Truly I say to you, you will not come out of there until you have paid up the last quadrans. ⁶⁰

~Jesus (Matthew 5:21-26 NASB)

<u>Anger at work is a huge issue</u>. We are challenged with it on a frequent basis. We express it in many ways. Our co-workers see it. They take note. Jesus challenges us to break the cycle.

<u>How do we break the cycle of anger at work?</u> Jesus shows us the way. Jesus shows us the way of love.

<u>Our mission at work</u>, given to us by Jesus, is to love. That is, it. That should be our day. That should be our motivation. Love should be our passionate focus at work. Love blunts anger completely.

> "Do not repay anyone evil for evil. Be careful to do what is right in the eyes of everybody. **If it is possible, as far as it depends on you, live at peace with everyone**… 'If your enemy is hungry, feed him; if he is thirsty, give him something to drink. In doing this you will hear

---

⁶⁰ *New American Standard Bible*. (2020). (Mt 5:21–26). La Habra, CA: The Lockman Foundation.

burning coals on his head.' Do not be overcome by evil but <u>overcome evil with good</u>."

(Romans 12:17-18, 20-21)

Should I renounce anger at work? Jesus does *not* exhort us to get angry, as if this is anger were a good motivator or energy for positive action. (This is the kind of thing that many Psychologists and "pop psychologists" in our culture today teach.) The context of Ephesians 4:25-32 is exactly the opposite! Paul is saying *when* you feel angry, do not act on it! Do not hold onto anger and do not let it motivate you because it easily leads to unwholesome talk and other sins. It gives the devil a foothold in your life. It grieves the Holy Spirit. It harms you and others. Instead of getting angry at people Paul teaches us to:

> ## <u>Be kind and compassionate to one another, forgiving each other, just as in the Messiah God forgave you.</u>

(Ephesians 4:32).

[Compassion Article: <u>Effective Leaders Move Beyond Empathy to Compassion (hbr.org)</u>]

"In your anger do not sin: Do not let the sun go down while you are still angry… Do not let any unwholesome talk come out of your mouths, but only what is helpful for building others up according to their needs, that it may help those who listen… **Get rid of all bitterness, rage, and anger, brawling and slander, along with every form of malice.** Be kind and compassionate to one another, forgiving each other, just as in the Messiah God forgave you." (Ephesians 4:26, 29 31-32)

Dealing with anger |' Becoming slow to anger: An honest reading of the Bible's wisdom on anger would never come away with this advice that anger is good! The consistent counsel in Scripture about anger is to be careful with it and to set it aside.

- 1 Corinthians 13:5 — Love does not act unbecomingly; it does not seek its own, **is not provoked**, does not consider a wrong suffered.
- Ecclesiastes 7:9 — **Do not be eager in your heart to be angry, For anger lives in the bosom of fools.**
- Titus 1:7 — For the overseer must be above reproach as God's steward, not self-willed, **not quick-tempered**, not addicted to wine, not pugnacious, not fond of sordid gain,
- James 1:19 — This you know, my beloved brethren. **But everyone must be quick to hear, slow to speak and slow to anger**.

Online Version: <u>Is anger at work dangerous for us? | Digital Business (wordpress.com)</u>

7.16 DEALING WITH WORKPLACE ROMANCES AND THE REAL ISSUE OF LUST FOR OUR CO-WORKERS.

> *You have heard that it was said, 'You shall not commit adultery;'*
> [28] *but I say to you that* **everyone who looks at a woman with lust for her has already committed adultery with her in his heart.**
> [29] *Now if your right eye is causing you to sin, tear it out and throw it away from you; for it is better for you to lose one of the parts of your body, than for your whole body to be thrown into ^hell.* [30] *And if your right hand is causing you to sin, cut it off and throw it away from you; for it is better for you to lose one of the parts of your body, than for your whole body to go into ^hell.* [61]

~Jesus (Matthew 5:27-30)

The workplace presents an unfortunate place for romance and affairs. We all know someone who is having an affair with someone at work. Lunches, happy hours, dinners, long hours, and frequency of contact create a willing environment for wandering.

Jesus frames it for us in a whole unusual way. As his disciples, we must deal with the real problem. We must deal with the real issue which is our lust. If we do not, it will lead to real problems at work. It could cost us our jobs.

Corporate Interest in solutions: Look at how much companies have spent on sexual harassment training and litigation. Jesus has a very straightforward solution.

This is an issue of our heart, but it does become a public issue at work if we are well known as a flirt, someone who puts women in awkward situations or harasses women. This is an issue that can ruin our testimony at work. This is an issue that can ruin our careers. This is an issue that can ruin our marriages. It happens too often.

What should we do? Jesus tells us to deal with the lust in our lives aggressively. "Tear it out" and "cut it off." Jesus is serious. We must get a handle on this. We need to have spiritual surgery and deal with the sources that lead us to lust at work.

- Do we look at pornography? Stop and tear it out of your life completely.
- Do certain TV shows cause our minds to wander? Do not watch them. Cut it off!

---

[61] *New American Standard Bible*. (2020). (Mt 5:27–30). La Habra, CA: The Lockman Foundation.

- Do we have friends that lead us astray in wrong thinking? Cut them out of our lives.
- Does attending certain functions, like "happy hours" and dinners create temptation in our lives? Cut out going to them when we can.
- Look at everything that is causing the lust and cut it out. Do it now. Be aggressive. Do not let it take hold of you.

We know that adultery begins with lust in our hearts. Jesus is clear about this. Scripture after scripture agrees. We must control ourselves. This is imperative for us at work.

- Proverbs 6:25 (ESV) —**Do not want her beauty in your heart, and do not let her capture you with her eyelashes.**
- Matthew 5:27–28 (ESV) — 27 "You have heard that it was said, 'You shall not commit adultery.' 28 **But I say to you that everyone who looks at a woman with lustful intent has already committed adultery with her in his hear**t.
- 2 Samuel 11:2–3 (ESV) — 2 It happened, late one afternoon, when David arose from his couch and was walking on the roof of the king's house, **that he saw from the roof a woman bathing; and the woman was exceptionally beautiful**. 3 And David sent and inquired about the woman. And one said, "Is not this Bathsheba, the daughter of Eliam, the wife of Uriah the Hittite?"
- Job 31:1 (ESV) — **"I have made a covenant with my eyes; how then could I gaze at a virgin?**
- Job 31:9 (ESV) — 9 "**If my heart has been enticed toward a woman**, and I have lain in wait at my neighbor's door,
- Jeremiah 5:8 (ESV) — 8 **They were well-fed, lusty stallions, each neighing for his neighbor's wife**.
- Matthew 15:19 (ESV) — 19 **For out of the heart come evil thoughts**, murder, **adultery**, sexual immorality, theft, false witness, slander.

Online Version: Dealing with workplace romances and the real issue of lust for our co-workers. | Digital Business (wordpress.com)

7.17 THE BENEFIT OF FAITHFULNESS IN MARRIAGE AT WORK

> *Now it was said, 'Whoever sends his wife away is to give her a certificate of divorce;' but **I say to you that everyone who divorces his wife, except for the reason of sexual immorality, makes her commit adultery; and whoever marries a divorced woman commits adultery**.*[62]

~Jesus (Matthew 5:31-32)

The way of Jesus, at work, is to prove our commitment to marriage and our families. There may be times we need to show that is our priority and takes precedence over work.

- Do our co-workers know of our commitment to our spouses?
- Will we be brave enough to balance our time between family and work?
- Will we honor others who show the same commitments?

Will we be tested? Yes, as we discussed in the earlier section, there is real temptation to violate our marriage vows. These two sections join as one. Lust leads to adultery. Adultery leads to broken marriages and families. That destroys any credibility for the message of Jesus in the workplace. If it happens, we must be honest and repent. It will not be easy.

What is the benefit here? We need more people of faith modeling healthy marriages and families at work. We spend so much time at work, our influence will spread in a significant way. Our co-workers will see it and say to themselves, "I want that."

Healthy families are the foundation of our culture. Time invested in building our families pays huge benefits over time to our way of living. This is important. How will our co-workers learn if we do not teach [as in discipling] them with how we do it the Jesus Way?

As followers of Jesus, there are other issues we will need to clear about.

- Marriage is between a man and woman.
- Men are men and women are women.
- Marriage is forever.

---

[62] *New American Standard Bible*. (2020). (Mt 5:31–32). La Habra, CA: The Lockman Foundation.

We are vulnerable, because he may attack us anew; but we are also victorious, because Jesus is on our side, helping us and building our characters. Psychologists tell us that violence is born of weakness, not strength. It is the strong man who can love and suffer hurt; it is the weak man who thinks only of himself and hurts others to protect himself. He hurts others then runs away to protect himself.

Avoiding the problem

It is all fine and good not to retaliate. That is the Way of Jesus. That should be our focus.

Is there a way to avoid even the need to?

- Romans 12:18 (CSB) — 18, If possible, as far as it depends on you, **live at peace with everyone**.
- 1 Peter 4:8 (CSB) — 8 Maintain **constant love for one another, since love covers a multitude of sins**.

Online Version: How should we handle our desires to retaliate at work? | Digital Business (wordpress.com)

7.20 IS LOVE ALL THAT MATTERS AT WORK?

> *"You have heard that it was said, 'you Shall love your neighbor and hate your enemy.'* [44] ***But I say to you, love your enemies and pray for those who persecute you,*** [45] *so that you may prove yourselves to be sons of your Father who is in heaven; for He causes His sun to rise on the evil and the good, and sends rain on the righteous and the unrighteous.* [46] *For if you love those who love you, what reward do you have? Even the tax collectors, do they not do the same?* [47] *And if you greet only your brothers and sisters, what more are you doing than others? Even the Gentiles, do they not do the same?* [48] *Therefore you shall be mature [perfect], as your heavenly Father is perfect.* [65]

~Jesus (Matthew 5:43-48)

Why it matters: We know we are supposed to love everyone at work. We are clear on that from Jesus. There is no doubt that is our goal.

And yet …

- We have enemies at work.
- Some of our co-workers hate us.
- We are persecuted for our faith.
- Vile and cruel things are said about us.

How will we really show our love at work? Jesus makes it clear that we way prove our love at work is for those who are our enemies. Love is not loving our supporters, those who champion our cause. Love is about loving those who oppose us, in demonstrable ways.

Some questions to ask ourselves:

- Do we speak well of the colleague who torpedoed our presentation last week?
- Do we go "the extra mile" to help another department leader who constantly trashes our departments work?

---

[65] *New American Standard Bible.* (2020). (Mt 5:43–48). La Habra, CA: The Lockman Foundation.

- Are we well known for showing mercy to the down and out team who purposefully tanks our joint project?

The way I see it: This is the tough thing to do at work. When our team goes after another "competing team," will we be willing to love them? Are we willing to put the time and effort into this, or will we put our heads in the sand hoping our love will not be tested? It is and will be tested. It will be tested every day. We have enemies at work. What will we do about it?

- Hide?
- Retaliate?
- Love, be kind, gentle and merciful?

We get to choose. Others are watching. Others are testing us just because they can.

Online version: Is love all that matters at work? | Digital Business (wordpress.com)

7.20.2   Is love a burden at work?

> *Everyone who believes that Jesus is the Messiah has been born of God, and everyone who loves the Father loves whoever has been born of him.* ***²By this we know that we love the children of God, when we love God and obey his commandments.*** *³For this is the love of God, that we keep his commandments.* ***And his commandments are not burdensome.*** ***⁴For everyone who has been born of God overcomes the world.*** *And this is the victory that has overcome the world—our faith.* *⁵Who is it that overcomes the world except the one who believes that Jesus is the Son of God?* [66]

1 John 5:3

The way I see it: I have always thought that loving other people at work is hard and difficult. I have been wrong. Faith in Jesus and the power of the Holy Spirit do not make love burdensome.

The Greek word for burdensome is βαρύςb, εῖα, ύ: about that which is difficult in view of its being burdensome— 'burdensome, troublous.'

- καὶ αἱ ἐντολαὶ αὐτοῦ βαρεῖαι οὐκ εἰσίν 'and his commandments are not burdensome' 1 Jn 5:3.
- In rendering 'his commandments are not burdensome,**'** **it may be necessary in some languages to translate 'it is not difficult to do what he has commanded**.'[67]

Why it matters: We are not victims. We are born of God and hence "overcome the world" and the way of the evil one. We are born to love our colleagues. And we will.

How to start and grow in love at work: If love is not a burden, and yet it feels that way to us, how do we get started? How do we grow?

Start with service of others at work: Jesus always challenges us to be servants and serve others. Jesus would say your focus in work is to be a servant and a slave. Always be last. Sacrifice and put others first. That is all there is to do. It never changes. When

---

[66] *The Holy Bible: English Standard Version* (Wheaton, IL: Crossway Bibles, 2016), 1 Jn 5:1–5.

[67] Johannes P. Louw and Eugene Albert Nida, *Greek-English Lexicon of the New Testament: Based on Semantic Domains* (New York: United Bible Societies, 1996), 245.

we do that, we will be made first. That may include what others call leadership positions. Our choice is to serve. Because of our service, others may choose to make us first. Jesus was quite explicit about the cost of following Him. Discipleship requires a totally committed life. We must be all in. We must give up everything for Jesus.

Move to compassion with our co-workers: Service always is love in action. Layered in with compassion and we see that love is not a burden. The chart below, while of a secular origin (HBR), is right on target. Is our focus on making sure we are here "to help." It is not a burden to have compassion and look to help our colleagues. It is a simple question to always ask: "How can I help you?"

Compassion Goes Beyond
Sympathy and Empathy

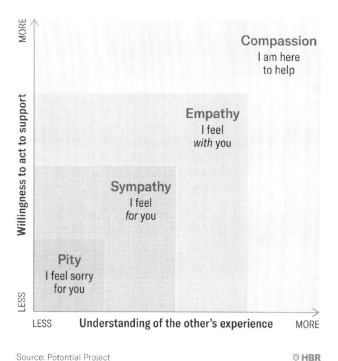

Source: Potential Project   ☕ HBR

Online Version: Is love a burden at work? | Digital Business (wordpress.com)

7.21 How giving are we at work?

> [1] *"Take care not to practice your righteousness in the sight of people, to be noticed by them; otherwise, you have no reward with your Father who is in heaven.*
>
> [2] *"So __when you give to the poor__, do not sound a trumpet before you, as the hypocrites do in the synagogues and on the streets, so that they will be praised by people. Truly I say to you, they have their reward in full.* [3] *But __when you give to the poor__, do not let your left hand know what your right hand is doing,* [4] *so that __your charitable giving will be in secret__; and your Father who sees what is done in secret will reward you.* [68]

~Jesus (Matthew 6:1-4)

__Are there any poor at work?__ Do we know them? Yes, there are poor people at work. Some do not make very much. Others have a huge burden of debt. They might be single parents struggling to pay for rent, childcare and get food on the table. They might have lost their house and are living in their car. They may have too much credit card debt and be on the verge of bankruptcy. They need help. What will we do?

__Do we seek them out at work?__ We can keep our eyes and ears open. Someone knows what is going on with them. Have we tapped into the network that can guide us to our co-workers in need?

__How does Jesus challenge us at work?__ Jesus said clearly "when you give." Jesus clearly expects us to do something for the poor.

__The bottom line:__ No matter how we help our co-workers, it is to be done in secret. No one should know what we are up to. Our reward is the joy of helping not adulation by others as a saint.

__God's goal for us at work:__ Jesus challenges us to be generous. Jesus expects us to help the poor at work. This is not optional. Are we known for being generous at work? When our colleagues know about someone who is struggling, do they think of us and ask us to help?

---

[68] *New American Standard Bible*. (2020). (Mt 6:1–4). La Habra, CA: The Lockman Foundation.

7.23 Is FASTING IMPORTANT IN THE WORKPLACE?

> *"Now **whenever you fast**, do not make a gloomy face as the hypocrites do, for they distort their faces so that they will be noticed by people when they are fasting. Truly I say to you, they have their reward in full. [17] But as for you, **when you fast**, anoint your head and wash your face, [18] **so that your fasting will not be noticed by people but by your Father who is in secret**; and your Father who sees what is done in secret will reward you.* [70]

~Jesus (Matthew 6:16-18)

Why it matters at work: We are to fast. Jesus expects it. We are to fast and pray. We are to fast and pray for our co-workers, our companies, and our supervisors, managers, and corporate officers. We are to do it at work. We are to do it in such a way that none of our colleagues know we are doing it.

Fasting may express our self-humbling before God. For if 'penitence and fasting' go together in Scripture, 'prayer and fasting' are even more often coupled. This is not so much a regular practice, so that whenever we pray, we fast, as an occasional and special arrangement, so that when we need to seek God for some direction or blessing, we turn aside from food and other distractions to do so.

Our Master Jesus himself fasted at once before his public ministry began; and the early church followed his example, the church of Antioch before Paul and Barnabas were sent out on the first missionary journey, and Paul and Barnabas themselves before appointing elders in every new church which they had planted. The evidence is plain that special enterprises need special prayer, and that special prayer may well involve fasting. We should regularly fast for our workplaces.

Hunger is one of our basic human appetites, and greed one of our basic human sins. So 'self-control' is meaningless unless it includes the control of our bodies and is impossible without self-discipline. Paul uses the athlete as his example. To compete in the games, he must be physically fit, and therefore he goes into training. His training will include a disciplined regime of food, sleep, and exercise: 'every athlete exercises self-control in all things.' This discipline is important at work. The discipline of fasting will show up in our discipline in the workplace. Our co-workers will see the fruit.

---

[70] *New American Standard Bible*. (2020). (Mt 6:16–18). La Habra, CA: The Lockman Foundation.

Followers of Jesus engaged in the race of faith at work should do the same. Paul writes of 'pommeling' his body (beating it black and blue) and 'subduing' it (leading it about as a slave). This is neither masochism (finding pleasure in self-inflicted pain), nor false asceticism (like wearing a hair shirt or sleeping on a bed of spikes), nor an attempt to win merit like the Pharisee in the temple. Paul would reject all such ideas, and so must we. We have no cause to 'punish' our bodies (for they are God's creation) but must discipline them to make them obey us. And fasting (a voluntary abstinence from food) is one way of increasing our self-control at work.

Online Version: Is fasting important in the workplace? | Digital Business (wordpress.com)

7.24 How do we break the hold money has on us at work?

> "**Do not store up for yourselves treasures on earth**, where moth and rust destroy, and where thieves break in and steal. But **store up for yourselves treasures in heaven**, where neither moth nor rust destroys, and where thieves do not break in or steal; for where your treasure is, there your heart will be also.
>
> "The eye is the lamp of the body; so then, if your eye is clear, your whole body will be full of light. But if your eye is bad, your whole body will be full of darkness. So, if the light that is in you is darkness, how great is the darkness!
>
> "**No one can serve two masters**; for either he will hate the one and love the other, or he will be devoted to one and despise the other. **You cannot serve God and wealth**. [71]

~Jesus (Matthew 6:19-24)

Why it matters at work: Most of us work for the primary purpose of making a living. We join companies because of the money. We leave companies because of the money. It is a huge driving force at work. We are manipulated day in and day out because of our salary and benefits. It will test our faith. Jesus is clear about this.

We are going to be out of step on with our co-workers this issue. We are not to concern ourselves with money at work. We are working to store up our heavenly wealth not our monthly salary in our jobs.

What? Jesus cannot be serious about this, can he?

- Jesus gives us a binary choice here. Serve God or money.
- Jesus knows the danger of materialism.
- This is a huge issue for us in our lives and will test our faith at work.

Money at work controls most corporate behavior. Companies and executives know this. We must break the hold money has on us at work and be free. That freedom will

---

[71] *New American Standard Bible*. (2020). (Mt 6:19–24). La Habra, CA: The Lockman Foundation.

7.26.1   What is the origin of hypocrisy at work?

Hypocrisy at work is a matter of our hearts. It comes through deceit, including deceit of ourselves. Our heart is naturally deceitful. That is the way it is, and we must own up to that. We are not always faithful to Jesus, even though we say we are. We will destroy our testimony through blatant hypocrisy at work.

The hypocrisy of our leaders: This is a huge issue in the corporate world. Reality dictates that often, our leaders are acting in bad faith and are real hypocrites. Want to be an effective leader? Flee from hypocrisy with ruthless transparency.

- "For from within, **out of the heart of men**, proceed the evil thoughts, fornications, thefts, murders, adulteries, deeds of coveting and wickedness, **as well as deceit,** sensuality, envy, slander, pride and foolishness." Mark 7:21–22

- Jeremiah 17:9 — **The heart is more deceitful than all else** and is desperately sick. Who can understand it?

- Hosea 10:2 — **Their heart is faithless**. Now they must bear their guilt. The Master will break down their altars and destroy their sacred pillars.

There is good news! Jesus has redeemed me and freed me from my deceitful heart. I am a new creation, pure and holy. I can be a straight shooter at work.

- Hebrews 10:22 — Let us draw near with a **sincere heart in full assurance of faith**, having our hearts sprinkled clean from an evil conscience and our bodies washed with pure water.

- James 3:17 — **But the wisdom from above is first pure**, then peaceable, gentle, reasonable, full of mercy and good fruits, unwavering, **without hypocrisy**.

Online Version: What is the origin of hypocrisy at work? | Digital Business (wordpress.com)

7.26.2   The expression of hypocrisy is through Insincere motives at work.

Hypocrisy at work is expressed in several ways. We have insincere motives, what we do is not aligned with what we say or think, and our tendency to consistently judge our colleagues. A constant theme here is, am I doing things for God or to get honor and praise from my boss and co-workers.

Avoiding public displays of religiosity is essential at work. As a friend of mine says, if you are going to publicly pray before the meal, you better be a good tipper. Our co-workers know that our piety is useless as we tear our co-workers down. Our judgmental attitude is a disconnect.

- Matthew 6:2 — "So when you give to the poor, do not sound a trumpet before you, **as the hypocrites do** in the synagogues and in the streets, so that they may be honored by men. Truly I say to you, they have their reward in full.

- Matthew 6:5 — "When you pray, **you are not to be like the hypocrites**; for they love to stand and pray in the synagogues and on the street corners so that they may be seen by men. Truly I say to you, they have their reward in full.

- Matthew 6:16 — "Whenever you fast, do not put on a gloomy face **as the hypocrites do**, for they neglect their appearance so that they will be noticed by men when they are fasting. Truly I say to you, they have their reward in full.

- Matthew 15:7–9 — "**You hypocrites, rightly did Isaiah prophesy of you**: 'This people honors Me with their lips, But their heart is far away from Me. 'But in vain do they worship Me, Teaching as doctrines the precepts of men.'"

- Matthew 22:18 — But **Jesus perceived their malice, and said, "Why are you testing Me, you hypocrites?** "

- Matthew 23:5–7 — "But **they do all their deeds to be noticed by men**; for they broaden their phylacteries and lengthen the tassels of their garments. They love the place of honor at banquets and the chief seats in the synagogues, and respectful greetings in the marketplaces, and being called Rabbi by men."

Online Version: The expression of hypocrisy is through Insincere motives at work. | Digital Business (wordpress.com)

7.26.3   The hypocrisy of corporate leaders is dangerous.

You hypocrite, first take the log out of your own eye, and then you will see clearly to take the speck out of your brother's eye.

Matthew 7:5

<u>**During Jesus' earthly ministry, He had many run-ins with the elites of the day,**</u> the Scribes, Pharisees, merchants, and businesspeople. These men were well versed in the Scriptures and zealous about following every letter of the work rules.

What would Jesus say today?

- **In adhering to the letter of rules**, they actively sought loopholes that allowed them to violate the spirit of why we have the rule.

- **The elites** displayed a lack of compassion toward their fellow man and were often overly demonstrative of their so-called spirituality to garner praise.

- **Jesus denounced their behavior** directly, pointing out that "justice, mercy, and faithfulness" are more important than pursuing a perfection based on faulty work standards.

- **Jesus made it clear** that the problem was not with the rules and policies but the way in which the elite leaders implemented them.

Today, the word pharisee has become synonymous with hypocrite. Translate it to the current religious and business elites. Some current day leaders (but not all by any means) are hypocrites. Warning! Beware!

- The prophet Isaiah condemned the hypocrisy of his day: "The Master says, 'These people come near to me with their mouth and honor me with their lips, but their hearts are far from me. Their worship of me is made up only of rules taught by men'" (Isaiah 29:13).

- Centuries later, Jesus quoted this verse, aiming the same condemnation at the religious leaders of His day (Matthew 15:8-9).

- John the Baptist refused to give hypocrites a pass, telling them to produce "fruits worthy of repentance" (Luke 3:8).

Jesus took an equally staunch stand against sanctimony at work.

He called religious leaders' hypocrites.

- "wolves in sheep's clothing" (Matthew 7:15)

- "whitewashed tombs" (Matthew 23:27)

- "snakes," and "brood of vipers" (Matthew 23:33).

Online Version: The hypocrisy of corporate leaders is dangerous. | Digital Business (wordpress.com)

7.27 ARE WE REALLY TREATING OTHERS AT WORK THE WAY WE WANT TO BE TREATED?

> *Ask, and it will be given to you; look for, and you will find; knock, and it will be opened to you. For everyone who asks receives, and the one who seeks finds, and to the one who knocks it will be opened. Or what person is there among you who, when his son asks for a loaf of bread, will give him a stone? Or if he asks for a fish, he will not give him a snake, will he? So, if you, despite being evil, know how to give good gifts to your children, how much more will your Father who is in heaven give good things to those who ask Him!*
>
> *"In everything, therefore, treat people the same way you want them to treat you, for this is the Law and the Prophets.* [73]

~Jesus (Matthew 7:7-12)

We all know the golden rule. My guess is that most of us agree with it. It is also my guess that most of us do not live it out daily at work. We want our co-workers to be nice and pleasant. Yet, we are mean and cruel, saying unkind things behind our co-workers' (or boss') backs.

Can we make this our habit at work? Jesus commands us to do this at work. Have we made it our habit? What would our action plan look like if worked on it every day? Are we ready for feedback from our colleagues and those who work for us? Can we suggest it as a development item for others, particularly if we supervise others?

The way I see it: This is the main thing about the main thing at work. Jesus says so. Jesus is clear. We must get clear on it as well. How would our work culture change if this were our primary focus? Would our customer engagement soar if we treated our customers like we want to be treated?

Consider this: Put this at the top of your to do list every day for a month. At the end of the day, last thing, assess how you did and add refinements to your to do list for the next day.

To Do:

- Treat people the same way you want them to treat you.

---

[73] *New American Standard Bible*. (2020). (Mt 7:7–12). La Habra, CA: The Lockman Foundation.

- That is, it.

The broad view: This will make an enormous difference. Just try it. Jesus knows what He is talking about, and your colleagues will thank you for it!

Online Version: Are we really treating others at work the way we want to be treated? | Digital Business (wordpress.com)

7.28 DO WE CHOOSE THE NARROW WAY AT WORK?

> *Enter through the narrow gate; for the gate is wide and the way is broad that leads to destruction, and there are many who enter through it. For the gate is narrow and the way is constricted that leads to life, and there are few who find it.* [74]

~Jesus (Matthew 7:13-14)

Why it matters at work: It seems like normally we like to take safety in numbers. We delight that in looking at opinion polls, we are in the majority. We go into denial when we are the minority. The reality is that most people at work will reject the Way of Jesus. We must be prepared to be in the minority opinion of our colleagues on most issues at work. This is not easy. Jesus knows that and alerts us to the reality of workplace opinions.

God is God at work: Our supervisors like to think that they and the corporate elites are in charge. That is the working premise. Most employees follow right along with that assumption. We like to follow along and fit in. That feels good to us. The counter reality is that Jesus is in charge and rules over corporate life.

- Rejecting God at work is dangerous to our souls.
- Rejecting God at work leads to our destruction.
- Jesus challenges us at work to follow the narrow way of the Way of Love.
- The Jesus way of love is the way that leads to life.

These are, of course, the way to heaven and the way to hell. The broad way is the effortless way; it is the trendy way at work. But we must not judge spiritual profession by statistics; the majority is not always right. The fact that "everybody does it" at work is no proof that what they are doing is right.

Quite the contrary is true at work: God's people have always been a remnant, a small minority in the corporate world. The reason is not difficult to discover: The way of life is narrow, lonely, and costly. We can walk on the broad way and keep our "baggage" of sin and worldliness. But if we enter the narrow way, we must give up those things.

Here, then, is the work test: Did your profession of faith in the Messiah cost you anything at your workplace? If not, then it is not a true profession. Many people who "trust" Jesus the Messiah never leave the broad road with its appetites and associations

---

[74] *New American Standard Bible.* (2020). (Mt 7:13–14). La Habra, CA: The Lockman Foundation.

with evil co-workers. They have an easy Christianity that makes no demands on them. Yet Jesus said that the narrow way was hard. We cannot walk on two roads, in two different directions at work, at the same time.

Online Version: Do we choose the narrow way at work? | Digital Business (wordpress.com)

7.29 WHAT KIND OF FRUIT ARE WE GROWING AT WORK?

> "Beware of the false prophets, who come to you in sheep's clothing, but inwardly are ravenous wolves. **¹⁶ You will know them by their fruits**. Grapes are not gathered from thorn bushes, nor figs from thistles, are they? ¹⁷ So every good tree bears good fruit, but the bad tree bears bad fruit. ¹⁸ A good tree cannot bear bad fruit, nor can a bad tree bear good fruit. ¹⁹ Every tree that does not bear good fruit is cut down and thrown into the fire. ²⁰ So then, you will know them by their fruits.
>
> ²¹ **"Not everyone who says to Me, 'Lord, Lord,' will enter the kingdom of heaven, but the one who does the will of My Father who is in heaven will enter.** ²² Many will say to Me on that day, 'Lord, Lord, did we not prophesy in Your name, and in Your name cast out demons, and in Your name perform many miracles?' ²³ And then I will declare to them, 'I never knew you; leave Me, you who practice lawlessness.' [75]

~Jesus (Matthew 7:15-23)

The way I see it: We have some genuine issues to deal with at work. Are others speaking the truth? We have lots of corporate leaders saying lots of things. There are plenty of business experts. Can we trust them?

Why it matters at work: Jesus shows us the way to figure things out. Jesus tells us to look at their fruit. The Apostle Pau helps us out here:

> **But the fruit of the Spirit is love, joy, peace, patience, kindness, goodness, faithfulness, gentleness, self-control**; against such things there is no law. [76]

God's goal: The goal is to be discerning at work and not just accept what others want us to believe.

---

[75] *New American Standard Bible*. (2020). (Mt 7:15–23). La Habra, CA: The Lockman Foundation.

[76] *The Holy Bible: English Standard Version* (Ga 5:22–23). (2016). Crossway Bibles.

- Is it said in love and lead to loving relationships?
- Does it bring peace into our lives?
- Is the business leader patient?
- Are the words ones of kindness, upholding the dignity of others?

It is all about growing and maturity. Are we growing in the following areas?

- Love
- Joy
- Peace
- Patience
- Kindness
- Goodness
- Faithfulness
- Gentleness
- Self-Control

This should keep our personal development plans packed with plenty to focus on every day.

Online Version: <u>What kind of fruit are we growing? | Digital Business (wordpress.com)</u>

7.30 HAPPINESS AND JOY

7.30.1   Happiness at work comes from keeping God's commands and being obedient.

The word *blessed* derives from the Greek term *makarios*, which means "fortunate," "happy," "enlarged," or "lengthy." *Makarios* is used in the Septuagint (a translation of the Old Testament into the Greek language) and the New Testament to define the kind of happiness that comes from receiving favor from God. Consequently, *blessed* can also be translated "favored." In the New Testament, it usually carries the meaning of being "blessed by God." As in the case of Mary, the mother of Jesus, who was "blessed among women" (Luke 1:42-45, 48), it was the Lord God who had blessed and favored her.

- Proverbs 29:18 — 18 Where there is no vision, the people are unrestrained, **But happy is he who keeps the law.**
- Isaiah 56:1–2 —Thus says the Master, "Preserve justice and do righteousness, For My salvation is about to come And My righteousness to be revealed. **How happy is the man who does this**, And the son of man who takes hold of it, Who keeps from profaning the sabbath, And keeps his hand from doing any evil."
- Matthew 24:46 (CSB) – "Happy is that servant whom the master finds doing his job when he comes."
- Luke 12:43 (CSB) – "Happy is that servant whom the master finds doing his job when he comes.

Happiness at work comes from God's word.

Are you ecstatically happy in your job?

- Luke 11:27–28 (NASB) —While Jesus was saying these things, one of the women in the crowd raised her voice and said to Him, "Happy is the womb that bore You and the breasts at which You nursed." But He said, "On the contrary, **happy are those who hear the word of God and observe it.**"
- The Greek word "ecstasy" (ἔκστασις, *ekstasis*) means "standing outside of" and refers to the experience of having the mind cut off from ordinary sense feelings. These experiences are often referred to as mystical or ecstatic experiences.
- Does Jesus amaze me? Am I stunned by His beauty and brilliance? Am I rejoicing in the Holy Spirit?
- Revelation 1:3 —**Happy is he who reads and those who hear the words of the prophecy, and heed** the things which are written in it; for the time is near.
- Revelation 22:7 — "And behold, I am coming quickly. **Happy is he who heeds the words of the prophecy of this book.**"

Happiness comes from the joyful sounds of God.

Psalm 89:15 — **How happy are the people who know the joyful sound**! O Master, they walk in the light of Your countenance.

We seem a little reluctant to talk about the ecstatic experience. Is that for mystics and weirdos, I think?

It is not just for kooks.

- Doesn't Jesus just rock my world?
- Am I out of my mind at what Jesus is doing?
- Am I crazy in love with Jesus?
- Am I stunned at His beauty and brilliance?

Psalm 100 Be Thankful -**A psalm of thanksgiving.** Let the whole earth shout triumphantly to the Lord! Serve the Lord with gladness; **come before him with joyful songs.**

Happiness at work comes from the discipline of God.

- Job 5:17 — "Behold, **how happy is the man whom God reproves**, So do not despise the discipline of the Almighty.
- Psalm 94:12 —**Happy is the man whom You chasten**, O Master, And whom You teach out of Your law.

Happiness at work comes from not being evil.

Psalm 1:1–2 —**How happy is the man who does not walk in the counsel of the wicked**, Nor stand in the path of sinners, Nor sit in the seat of scoffers! But his delight is in the law of the Master, And in His law, he meditates day and night.

Happiness at work comes from the fear of God.

- Hebrews 12: 2 -- For the **joy** that lay **before him**, he endured the cross, despising the shame, and sat down at the right hand of the throne of God.
- Psalm 112:1 —Praise the Master! **How happy is the man who fears the Master**, Who delights in His commandments.
- Psalm 128:1 —**How happy is everyone who fears the Master**, Who walks in His ways.
- Proverbs 28:14 —**How happy is the man who fears always**, But he who hardens his heart will fall into calamity.

Online version: Happiness at work comes from keeping God's commands and being obedient. | Digital Business (wordpress.com)

7.30.2   Do God's people find their joy at work in Jesus?

Jesus wants me to glad, joyful and happy in my work. Jesus paid the price for my missing God's goal (aka sin). I deserved death. Jesus died in my place. Jesus is resurrected and sits in authority next to God as King of God's country. That should make me glad. If it does not, what is wrong with me?

The Apostle Paul is emphatic in Philippians 3. He says "rejoice" and then he emphatically says it again. The word here is χαίρω (chairó). It means to be glad, happy and rejoice. It comes to us by combining. xará ("joy") and xáris ("grace").

God has put gladness in the hearts of the disciples of Jesus at work. It is much better than any food or drink. It is a pure gift to all of us. What a God we serve!

- Philippians 4:4 — **Rejoice** in the Master always; **again, I will say, rejoice**!
- Psalm 4:7 — 7 **You have put gladness in my heart**, More than when their grain and new wine abound.
- Habakkuk 3:17–18 — 17 Though the fig tree should not blossom And there be no fruit on the vines, Though the yield of the olive should fail And the fields produce no food, Though the flock should be cut off from the fold And there be no cattle in the stalls, 18 Yet **I will exult in the Master, I will rejoice in the God of my salvation**.
- Philippians 3:1 — 1 Finally, my brethren**, rejoice in the Master**. To write the same things again is no trouble to me, and it is a safeguard for you.

- 1 Chronicles 16:10 — 10 Glory in His holy name; **Let the heart of those who seek the Master be glad**.

- Psalm 43:4 — 4 Then I will go to the altar of God, **To God my exceeding joy**; And upon the lyre I shall praise You, O God, my God.

- Philippians 1:23–26 — 23 But I am hard-pressed from both directions, having the desire to leave and be with the Messiah, for that is very much better; 24 yet to remain on in the flesh is more necessary for your sake. 25 Convinced of this, I know that I will remain and continue with you all for your progress and **joy in the faith**, 26 so that your proud confidence in me may abound in the Messiah Jesus through my coming to you again.

Online version: Do God's people find their joy at work in Jesus? | Digital Business (wordpress.com)

7.30.3   Does God himself give joy to us at work?

The joy I have, in Jesus my Master, is a gift from God. I do not screw up my courage and become happy automatically. Of course, I must decide to accept it. Gifts are not gifts if they are not received. Having the joy of Master Jesus at work is huge.

We also know that joy is one of the fruits of the Holy Spirit. Fruit goes through a growing process, from seed to tree to fruit. It must be cultivated. There is a role for me at work there as well.

The "fruit of the Spirit" is what happens when the Holy Spirit indwells a believer. The "fruit" is the product of the Holy Spirit's cultivation of character in the heart. Galatians 5:22-23 describes what that fruit looks like; the second characteristic listed is joy.

For the kingdom of God is not eating and drinking, but righteousness and peace and joy in the Holy Spirit. (Romans 14:17).

- Nehemiah 12:43 — 43 and on that day, they offered great sacrifices and **rejoiced because God had given them immense joy**, even the women and children rejoiced, so that the joy of Jerusalem was heard from afar.
- 2 Chronicles 20:27–28 – 27 Then all the men of Judah and Jerusalem turned back with Jehoshaphat their leader, returning joyfully to Jerusalem, **for the Lord enabled them to rejoice over their enemies**. 28 So they came into Jerusalem to the Lord's temple with harps, lyres, and trumpets.
- Job 8:21 — 21 "**He will yet fill your mouth with laughter** and your lips with shouting."
- Ecclesiastes 2:26 — 26 For to a person who is good in His sight **He has given** wisdom, knowledge, and **joy**, while to the sinner He has given the task of gathering and collecting so that he may give to one who is good in God's sight. This too is vanity and striving after wind.
- Isaiah 9:3 — 3 You shall multiply the nation, **You shall increase their gladness**; They will be glad in Your presence As with the gladness of harvest, As men rejoice when they divide the spoil.

- Acts 13:52 — 52 And the disciples were continually filled with **joy** and with the Holy Spirit.

- Acts 14:15–17 — 15 and saying, "Men, why are you doing these things? We are also men of the same nature as you and preach the gospel to you that you should turn from these vain things to a living God, who made the heaven and the earth and the sea and all that is in them. 16 "In the generations gone by He allowed all the nations to go their own ways; 17 and yet He did not leave Himself without witness, in that He did good and gave you rains from heaven and fruitful seasons, **satisfying your hearts with food and gladness**

For discussion:

- How does the world define happiness?

- How does Jesus define happiness?

- What are the implications of the Jesus way for our faith at work?

- What are the implications of the Jesus way for leadership?

Online Version: Does God himself give joy to us at work? | Digital Business (wordpress.com)

8 WHAT IS OUR ROLE IN MAKING DISCIPLES OF JESUS AT WORK?

> *The eleven disciples traveled to Galilee, to the mountain where Jesus had directed them. When they saw him, they worshipped, but some doubted it. Jesus came near and said to them, "All authority has been given to me in heaven and on earth. **Go, therefore, and make disciples of all nations, baptizing them in the name of the Father and of the Son and of the Holy Spirit, teaching them to see everything I have commanded you.** And remember, I am with you always, to the end of the age."*

Matthew 28:16-20

What is a disciple? Is it relevant at work? A disciple is a student, pupil, or learner. In the New Testament it is used for Jesus' followers. Often references "the Twelve" but also shows a wider group of followers. This is important for our focus on our mission for Jesus at work. Are we focused on making disciples for Jesus? If not, why not?

In the New Testament, the term "disciple" is used in the Gospels and Acts. In most instances it is a technical term in reference to a follower of Jesus, although John the Baptist, the Pharisees, and Paul are also said to have disciples. In John, a group of Jews call themselves the disciples of Moses (John 9:28).

In the Gospels, Jesus creates His own group of disciples by calling individuals to follow Him. He also calls disciples that do not seem to qualify for the task (e.g., Matthew who is a tax collector—an occupation that was shunned and considered sinful in the land of Israel). At work, we follow the Way of Jesus. We are His disciples. The way we work is a clear reflection of what we learn from Jesus.

The development of the Jesus movement at work, the term disciple becomes synonymous with those who believe and confess that Jesus is the Messiah. This is reflected in Acts, where the term regularly refers to a believer in the Messiah, regardless of whether one had known Jesus during His earthly ministry.

Online Version: What is our role in making disciples of Jesus at work? | Digital Business (wordpress.com)

8.1 WHY IS MAKING DISCIPLES AT WORK IMPORTANT?

The making of disciples at work is our Master's means for answering the prayer, *"Our Father in heaven, hallowed be Your name, Your kingdom come, Your will be done on earth [at work] as it is in heaven"* (Matthew 6:9-10). In His infinite wisdom, Jesus chose to use dedicated followers, His disciples, to carry the message of salvation and Kingdom living to our colleagues at work. Our time at work is framed by how we do at making disciples. That is the mission we have from Jesus.

He included this as a command in His last words before His ascension to heaven:

> *"All authority in heaven and on earth has been given to Me. Therefore, **go and make disciples of all nations**, baptizing them in the name of the Father and of the Son and of the Holy Spirit, and teaching them to obey everything I have commanded you. And surely, I am with you always, to the very end of the age."*

(Matthew 28:18-20).

Making disciples at work is important because it is the Master's chosen method of spreading the Good News of salvation through Jesus the Messiah. During His public ministry, Jesus spent more than three years making disciples—teaching and training His chosen twelve. He gave them many convincing proofs that He was the Son of God, the promised Messiah; they believed on Him, though imperfectly. He spoke to the crowds, but often He drew the disciples aside privately to teach them the meaning of His parables and miracles. We must do the same at work. Discipleship at work is a huge opportunity.

Jesus sent them out on ministry assignments. He also taught them that soon He would be returning to His Father following His death and resurrection. Though they could not understand it, He made the disciples this astonishing promise:

> *"I tell you the truth, anyone who has faith in Me will do what I have been doing. He will do even greater things than these because I am going to the Father."*

(John 14:12).

Jesus also promised to send His Spirit to be with them forever at work.

Online Version: Why is making disciples at work important? | Digital Business (wordpress.com)

8.2 How we help co-workers to help others to follow Jesus.

> "To be human is to be a disciple. God did not present Adam and Eve with a choice between discipleship and independence, but between following him and following Satan. We are all disciples; the only question is, of whom?"
>
> ~ Mark Dever – Book "Discipling: How to Help Others Follow Jesus"

Jesus says discipleship is about "<u>teaching disciples to observe everything I have commanded you.</u>" What has Jesus commanded us to do at work?

> "Teacher, which command in the law is the greatest?" He said to him, **"Love the Lord your God with all your heart, with all your soul, and with all your mind.** This is the greatest and most important command.
>
> The second is like it: **Love your [colleagues] neighbor as yourself.** All the Law and the Prophets depend on these two commands."

"Love initiates a discipling relationship at work."

- Am I willing to start intentional time together with this person?
- Beyond starting the relationship, will I mention the hard conversation we need to have?
- Am I bold enough to consistently move our conversation to spiritual things?

"Love perseveres in a discipling relationship with our colleagues."

- Am I ready to keep calling after months of seeing little fruit or progress?
- Will I give up if this person falls back into an old pattern of sin?
- How will I respond to the inconveniences in this relationship?

"Love humbly receives criticism that often comes in a discipling relationship."

- How do I respond to criticism or opposition in general at work — with humility or pride?
- Specifically, what will I feel or say when this person pushes back on what I am teaching them?

- What healthy ways am I encouraging give-and-take in this relationship?

"Love humbly gives of itself in a discipling relationship."

- What sacrifices am I making to spend time discipling this person?

- Do I tend to feel bitter or prideful about the sacrifices I make for others?

- Jesus says, "It is more blessed to give than to receive" (Acts 20:35). Can I say the same?

"Love allows us to end discipling relationships."

- We need a love that humbles us enough to recognize that what others need is not us, but God, and that God can use us for a while, and then use someone else.

- Do I think of myself as savior or as one instrument among many in the Savior's hands?

- How do I think about my role in this person's life — as essential and irreplaceable, or as complementary and temporary?

- Am I willing to help move this person on to other teachers when their needs or circumstances suggest it is time? To that end, it may be wise to prove a clear time up front (e.g., a month, a year, two years), so that neither person assumes the disciplining relationship is indefinite.

Online Version: <u>How we help co-workers to help others to follow Jesus. | Digital Business (wordpress.com)</u>

8.3 WHY DOES JESUS WANT US TO MAKE DISCIPLES AT WORK?

As promised, on the Day of Pentecost, the Holy Spirit came with power over the believers, who then were emboldened to speak the Good News to everyone. The rest of the Book of Acts gives the exciting account of all that was carried out through them. In one city the opposition said, "These who have turned the world upside down are come here also" (Acts 17:6).

Multitudes placed their faith in Jesus the Messiah, and they also became disciples. Is that happening where we work? When strong persecution came from the false religious leaders, they dispersed to other areas and continued to obey the Messiah's command. Churches were set up throughout the Roman Empire, and eventually in other nations.

Later, because of disciples such as Martin Luther and others, Europe was opened to the Good News of Jesus the Messiah through the Reformation. Eventually, Christians emigrated to the Americas to make the Messiah known. Though the world still is not completely evangelized, the challenge is as doable now as ever before. Too long, we have avoided this issue at work. We have disconnected the mission of Jesus at work. We can no longer. We must be light.

The command of our Master is still – "Go and make disciples [at work], baptizing them, and teaching them to obey everything I have commanded you." The characteristics of a disciple of Jesus at work may be simply said as

- One who is assured of his salvation (John 3:16) and is activated by the indwelling Holy Spirit (John 14:26-27).

- One who is growing in the grace and knowledge of our Master and Savior (2 Peter 3:18); and

- One who shares the Messiah's burden for the lost souls of men and women. Jesus said, "The harvest is plentiful, but the workers are few. Ask the Master of the harvest, therefore, to send out workers into His harvest field" (Matthew 9:37-38).

Online Version: Why is making disciples in the workplace important? | Digital Business (wordpress.com)

8.4 WHAT IS THE COST OF DISCIPLESHIP AT WORK?

Jesus was quite explicit about the cost of following Him. Discipleship requires a totally committed life: Our focus at work is to focus on discipleship. At work, discipleship will cost us everything, not just a little.

> *"Any of you who does not give up everything he has cannot be my disciple."*

(Luke 14:33)

Sacrifice is expected: *"Jesus said to his disciples, 'If anyone would come after me, he must deny himself and take up his cross and follow me'"* (Matthew 16:24). Jesus is my Master. I am His slave. That is the demand of discipleship.

Not all of Jesus' followers were able to make such a commitment. There were many who left Jesus after a while. **"From this time many of his disciples turned back and no longer followed him"** (John 6:66).

The cost of discipleship involves a denial of all my self-interests and desires at work: Jesus' followers were called "disciples" long before they were ever called "the Christians." Their discipleship began with Jesus' call and required them to exercise their will to follow Him (Matthew 9:9).

Jesus demanded disciples become slaves of the Master (aka Owner). This is not optional even though it sounds repugnant. I am a slave of Jesus. I am totally devoted to Him.

- Matthew 16:24 — Then Jesus said to His disciples, **"If anyone wishes to come after Me, he must deny himself, and take up his cross and follow Me."**
- Matthew 10:38 — **"And he who does not take his cross and follow after Me is not worthy of Me."**
- Luke 14:27 — **"Whoever does not carry his own cross and come after Me cannot be My disciple."**

As a disciple, am I learning from Jesus? The Greek term for "disciple" in the New Testament is mathetes, which means more than just "student" or "learner." A disciple is a "follower," someone who adheres completely to the teachings of another, making them his rule of life and conduct. The Pharisees prided themselves in being disciples of Moses (John 9:28). Are we proud of being a disciple of Jesus at work? Is that clear to others?

Self-denial means leaders live for others at work.

- Romans 14:7 — 7 For not one of us lives for himself, and not one dies for himself.
- 2 Corinthians 5:15 — 15 and He died for all, so that they who live might no longer live for themselves, but for Him who died and rose again on their behalf.

- Galatians 2:20 — 20 "I have been crucified with the Messiah; and it is no longer I who live, but the Messiah lives in me; and the life which I now live in the flesh I live by faith in the Son of God, who loved me and gave Himself up for me.
- 1 Peter 4:2 — 2 to live the rest of the time in the flesh no longer for the lusts of men, but for the will of God.

Online Version: What is the cost of discipleship at work? | Digital Business (wordpress.com)

8.5 DISCIPLES IN THE WORKPLACE ARE ABUNDANTLY REWARDED IN THIS LIFE

<u>We are committed to being a disciple of Jesus at work.</u> It is clear to us and clear to others. The way we understand work, there is some reward associated with our work. Our faith in Jesus at work has its rewards.

<u>Jesus is clear</u> that we will benefit in this present age and at work. He does not waffle on this. He is also clear we will have eternal life in ages to come as well. When we live out our faith at work, we receive rewards now and in the future. How good is that?

God is good! Does our faith at work reflect that? Do our colleagues see it in our lives?

- **Mark 10:29–30** — **29** Jesus said, "<u>Truly I say to you, there is no one who has left house or brothers or sisters or mother or father or children or farms, for My sake and for the gospel's sake, 30 but that he will receive a hundred times as much now in the present age</u>, houses and brothers and sisters and mothers and children and farms, along with persecutions; and **in the age to come**, eternal life.

- **Matthew 7:7–11** — **7** "<u>Ask, and it will be given to you; seek, and you will find; knock, and it will be opened to you</u>. **8** "For everyone who asks receives, and he who seeks finds, and to him who knocks it will be opened. **9** "Or what man is there among you who, when his son asks for a loaf, will give him a stone? **10** "Or if he asks for a fish, he will not give him a snake, will he? **11** "If you then, being evil, know how to give good gifts to your children, **how much more will your Father who is in heaven give what is good to those who ask Him!**

- **John 8:12** — **12** Then Jesus again spoke to them, saying, "<u>I am the Light of the world; he who follows Me will not walk in the darkness, but will have the Light of life.</u>"

- **John 10:27** — **27** "My sheep hear My voice, and I know them, and they follow Me.

- **John 12:26** — **26** "<u>If anyone serves Me, he must follow Me; and where I am, there My servant will be also; if anyone serves Me, the Father will honor him.</u>

- **Romans 8:31–39** — **31** What then shall we say to these things? **If God is for us, who is against us?** **32** He who did not spare His own Son, but delivered Him over for us all, how will He not also with Him freely give us all things? **33** Who will bring a charge against God's elect? God is the one who justifies; **34** who is the one who condemns? the Messiah Jesus is He who died, yes, who was raised, who is at the right hand of God, who also intercedes for us. **35** Who will separate us from the love of the Messiah? Will tribulation, distress, persecution, famine, or nakedness, or peril, or sword? **36** Just as it is written, "For Your sake we are being put to death all day long; We were considered as sheep to be slaughtered." **37** <u>But in all these things we overwhelmingly conquer through</u>

Him who loved us. 38 For I am convinced that neither death, nor life, nor angels, nor principalities, nor things present, nor things to come, nor powers, **39** nor height, nor depth, nor any other created thing, **will be able to separate us from the love of God, which is in the Messiah Jesus our Master.**

- **1 Timothy 6:6 — 6 But godliness is a means of great gain when accompanied by contentment.**

Online version:

8.6 DISCIPLES AT WORK ARE HAPPY BY BEING UNITED WITH JESUS IN THE FAMILY OF GOD

At work, it is important to have friends. As disciples of Jesus, we go way beyond that. We are a part of the family of God. Our faith colleagues are our brothers and sisters.

The "Jesus Way" goal for our faith at work: Jesus sets our focus. It is to "do the will of His Father in heaven." When we do the will of God, we have a family at work. We align with the family of God at work.

- Matthew 12:46–50 — 46 While He was still speaking to the crowds, behold, His mother and brothers were standing outside, seeking to speak to Him. 47 Someone said to Him, "Behold, Your mother and Your brothers are standing outside seeking to speak to You." 48 But Jesus answered the one who was telling Him and said, "Who is My mother and who are My brothers?" 49 **And stretching out His hand toward His disciples, He said, "Behold My mother and My brothers! 50 "For whoever does the will of My Father who is in heaven, he is My brother and sister and mother."**
- Galatians 6:10 — 10 So then, while we have opportunity, let us do good to all people, and **especially to those who are of the household of the faith.**
- Ephesians 2:19 — 19 So then you are no longer strangers and aliens, but you are fellow citizens with the saints, and **are of God's household,**
- Ephesians 3:15 — 15 **from whom every family in heaven and on earth derives its name,**

God can do anything: Here is the good news. God has chosen to adopt us into His family. He does not have to, but He has. As a result of the power of God, we have brothers and sisters. We are a family at work. We must act like it.

Online Version: Disciples at work are happy by being united with Jesus in the family of God. | Digital Business (wordpress.com)

8.7 DISCIPLES WILL BE HAPPY AT WORK WITH ETERNAL LIFE

> *"All authority in heaven and on earth has been given to Me.*
> *Therefore, **go and make disciples of all nations**, baptizing them in*
> *the name of the Father and of the Son and of the Holy Spirit, and*
> *teaching them to obey everything I have commanded you. And*
> *surely, I am with you always, to the very end of the age."*

(Matthew 28:18-20).

Why this is important: As disciples of Jesus at our workplaces, we will happy knowing we have eternal life. That is our guarantee from Jesus. That confidence gives courage and hope. Both are essential in our "faith walk" at work. Our colleagues will see it and want the same in their lives.

When the Bible speaks of eternal life, it refers to a gift of God that comes only "through Jesus the Messiah our Master" (Romans 6:23). This gift contrasts with the "death" that is the natural result of sin.

The gift of eternal life comes to those who believe in Jesus the Messiah, who is Himself "the resurrection and the life" (John 11:25). The fact that this life is "eternal" shows that it is perpetual life—it goes on and on and on, with no end. When we have this assurance, our colleagues will notice.

It is a mistake, however, to view eternal life as simply an unending progression of years. A common New Testament word for "eternal" is aiónios, which carries the idea of quality at work as well as quantity. In fact, eternal life is not really associated with "years" at all, as it is independent of time. Eternal life can function outside of and beyond time, as well as within time.

For this reason, eternal life can be thought of as something that Christians experience at work now. Believers do not have to "wait" for eternal life, because it is not something that starts when they die. Rather, eternal life begins the moment a person exercises faith in Jesus. It is our current possession. John 3:36 says, "Whoever believes in the Son has eternal life." Note that the believer at work "has" (present tense) this life (the verb is present tense in the Greek, too). We find similar present-tense constructions in John 5:24 and John 6:47. The focus of eternal life is not on our future, but on our current standing in Christ.

- Matthew 19:29 — 29 "And everyone who has left houses or brothers or sisters or father or mother or children or farms for My name's sake, **will receive many times as much, and will inherit eternal life.**
- Matthew 25:46 — 46 "These will go away into eternal punishment, but the **righteous into eternal life.**"
- Romans 2:7 — 7 to those who by **perseverance in doing good seek for glory, honor, and immortality, eternal life.**

- Galatians 6:8 — 8 For the one who sows to his own flesh will from the flesh reap corruption, but **the one who sows to the Spirit will from the Spirit reap eternal life**.
- 1 John 1:2 — 2 and the life was manifested, and we have seen and testify and **proclaim to you the eternal life**, which was with the Father and was manifested to us—
- 1 John 5:11 — 11 And the testimony is this, **that God has given us eternal life, and this life is in His Son**.
- 1 John 5:13 — 13 These things I have written to you who believe in the name of the Son of God, so that **you may know that you have eternal life**.
- 1 John 5:20 — 20 And we know that the Son of God has come and has given us understanding so that we may know Him who is true; and we are in Him who is true, in His Son Jesus the Messiah. **This is the true God and eternal life**.

Online version: Disciples will be happy at work with eternal life | Digital Business (wordpress.com)

8.8 Disciples have the hope of being like Jesus at work.

What is the cost of discipleship at work?

- Jesus was quite explicit about the cost of following Him. Discipleship requires a totally committed life: ***"Any of you who does not give up everything he has cannot be my disciple"*** (Luke 14:33).
- Not all of Jesus' followers were able to make such a commitment. There were many who left Jesus after a while. **"From this time many of his disciples turned back and no longer followed him"** (John 6:66).

The cost of discipleship in the corporate world involves a denial of all my self-interests and desires: Jesus' followers were called "disciples" long before they were ever called "the Christians." Their discipleship began with Jesus' call and required them to exercise their will to follow Him (Matthew 9:9).

- 1 John 3:2 — 2 Beloved, now we are children of God, and it has not appeared yet what we will be. **We know that when He appears, we will be like Him, because we will see Him just as He is**.
- John 12:26 — 26 "If anyone serves Me, **he must follow Me**; and where I am, there My servant will be also; if anyone serves Me, the Father will honor him.
- John 14:3 — 3 "If I go and prepare a place for you, I will come again and receive you to Myself, **that where I am, there you may be also.**
- Romans 8:29 — 29 For those whom He foreknew, He also predestined to become conformed to the image of His Son, **so that He would be the firstborn among many brethren**.
- 1 Corinthians 15:49 — 49 Just as we have borne the image of the earthy**, we will also bear the image of the heavenly.**
- 2 Peter 1:4 — 4 For by these **He has granted to us His precious and magnificent promises, so that by them you may become partakers of the divine nature,** having escaped the corruption that is in the world by lust.

Jesus demanded disciples become slaves of the Master (aka Owner). This is not optional even though it sounds repugnant. I am a slave of Jesus. I am totally devoted to Him.

- Matthew 16:24 — Then Jesus said to His disciples, **"If anyone wishes to come after Me, he must deny himself, and take up his cross and follow Me."**
- Matthew 10:38 — **"And he who does not take his cross and follow after Me is not worthy of Me."**
- Luke 14:27 — **"Whoever does not carry his own cross and come after Me cannot be My disciple."**

As a disciple, am I learning from Jesus at work? The Greek term for "disciple" in the New Testament is mathetes, which means more than just "student" or "learner." A disciple is a "follower," someone who adheres completely to the teachings of another, making them his rule of life and conduct. The Pharisees prided themselves in being disciples of Moses (John 9:28).

Are we ready to leave everything to follow Jesus? Can we challenge our colleagues to do the same?

- **Matthew 4:19 — 19** And He said to them, "Follow Me, and I will make you fishers of men."
- **Matthew 8:18–22 — 18** Now when Jesus saw a crowd around Him, He gave orders to leave to the other side of the sea. **19** Then a scribe came and said to Him, "Teacher, I will follow You wherever You go." **20** Jesus said to him, "The foxes have holes and the birds of the air have nests, but the Son of Man has nowhere to lay His head." **21** Another of the disciples said to Him, "Master, permit me first to go and bury my father." **22** But Jesus said to him, "Follow Me, and allow the dead to bury their own dead."
- **Matthew 9:9 — 9** As Jesus went on from there, He saw a man called Matthew, sitting in the tax collector's booth; and He said to him, "Follow Me!" And he got up and followed Him.

Happiness results obedient discipleship

Jesus asks very penetrating questions of me. Jesus is <u>patient</u>. Jesus is waiting for my answer. What will I say?

> ***"Why do you call me, 'Master, Master,' and do not do what I say?"***

~Jesus | Luke 6:46

Jesus continues. *"As for <u>everyone who comes to me and hears my words and puts them into practice</u>, I will show you what they are like. They are like a man building a house, who dug down deep and laid the foundation on rock. When a flood came, the torrent struck that house but could not shake it, because it was well built. But <u>the one who hears my words and does not put them into practice </u>is like a man who built a house on the ground without a foundation. The moment the torrent struck that house, it collapsed, and its destruction was complete."*

In some circles, the end game is to be saved. Now that is important, but it is not the end game. Jesus outlines three steps:

1. Come to Him (be saved)

2. Hear his words (listen)

3. Put them into practice (act and do)

Jesus is waiting on my answer! What will I answer? I must say, I listen to you Master, and I will do what you ask! <u>Obedience</u> is critical.

That is authentic.

There is more! Our culture places a terrific value on happiness. We are just mistaken on how to get it. Happiness comes from obeying Jesus. That is, it.

Do I believe that? Will I, do it?

- Luke 11:28 — But Jesus said, "On the contrary, **happy are those who hear the word of God and observe it**."
- Proverbs 8:32 — "Now therefore, O sons, listen to me, For **happy are they who keep my ways.**
- Matthew 7:24–25 — "Therefore everyone who hears these words of Mine and acts on them, may be compared to a wise man who built his house on the rock. "And the rain fell, and the floods came, and the winds blew and slammed against that house; and yet it did not fall, for it had been founded on the rock.
- John 13:17 — "**If you know these things, you are happy if you do them.** "
- John 14:21 — "**He who has My commandments and keeps them is the one who loves Me;** and he who loves Me will be loved by My Father, and I will love him and will disclose Myself to him."
- James 1:25 — But one who looks intently at the perfect law, the law of liberty, and abides by it, not having become a forgetful hearer but an effectual doer, this man will be happy in what he does.

Online Version: <u>Disciples have the hope of being like Jesus at work and being with him in heaven | Digital Business (wordpress.com)</u>

8.9 DISCIPLESHIP INCLUDES PERSECUTION AT WORK

Are we ready to be persecuted at work? Jesus has a promise for us. We will be. We must be ready.

- Are we ready to be fired?
- Are we ready to have complaints filed against us from Human Resources?
- Are we ready to be sued and taken to court?
- Are we ready?

But you are thinking, hmm, **no one is persecuting me at work**. That is true for many Christians I know at work. This is a problem and indicative that we are not living out our faith at work. This is a warning. Please take it seriously.

- John 15:20 — 20 "Remember the word that I said to you, 'A slave is not greater than his master.' **If they persecuted Me, they would also persecute you; if they kept My word, they would keep yours also**.
- Acts 14:22 — 22 strengthening the souls of the disciples, encouraging them to continue in the faith, and saying, **"Through many tribulations we must enter the kingdom of God."**
- 2 Timothy 3:12 — 12 **Indeed, all who want to live godly in the Messiah Jesus will be persecuted.**

Online Version: Discipleship includes persecution at work. | Digital Business (wordpress.com)

WHAT IS WORK?

God ordained work as the normal routine of living. Every legitimate human task, therefore, is of intrinsic worth, however menial it may seem, and is potentially a means of glorifying God. We all get the opportunity to live out our Faith at Work. That is the way of Jesus.

8.10 PEACE RESULTS FROM DISCIPLESHIP AT WORK

Why it matters: We all want peace. Considering how much time we spend at work; we want peace at work and with our colleagues. Our well-being is at stake. Our health is too important to ignore this. And yet, we do. What is up with that?

The "Jesus Way" goal for our faith at work: To have peace, we must be peacemakers. Jesus explicitly challenges to do exactly that. We are always an advocate for peace.

Good news: Peace comes from Jesus. He paid the price so that we could have peace with our Father in heaven. It is a gift. We have done nothing at all to earn it. We must make that clear to our colleagues.

- John 14:27 — 27 "**Peace I leave with you; My peace I give to you; not as the world gives do I give to you.** Do not let your heart be troubled, nor let it be fearful.
- Matthew 11:28–29 — 28 "**Come to Me, all who are weary and heavy-laden, and I will give you rest.** 29 "Take My yoke upon you and learn from Me, for I am gentle and humble in heart, and you will find rest for your souls.
- Luke 2:14 — 14 "Glory to God in the highest, **And on earth peace among men with whom He is pleased.**"
- Luke 24:36 — 36 While they were telling these things, He Himself stood in their midst and said to them, **"Peace be to you."**
- John 20:19 — 19 So when it was evening on that day, the first day of the week, and when the doors were shut where the disciples were, for fear of the Jews, Jesus came and stood in their midst and said to them, **"Peace be with you."**
- John 16:33 — 33 **"These things I have spoken to you, so that in Me you may have peace.** In the world you have tribulation but take courage; I have overcome the world."
- John 20:21 — 21 So Jesus said to them again, **"Peace be with you; as the Father has sent Me, I also send you."**
- John 20:26 — 26 After eight days His disciples were again inside, and Thomas with them. Jesus came, the doors having been shut, and stood in their midst and said, **"Peace be with you."**

- Numbers 6:26 — 26 The Master lift His countenance on you And **give you peace.'**
- Psalm 4:8 — 8 **In peace I will both lie down and sleep,** For You alone, O Master, make me dwell in safety.
- Psalm 29:11 — 11 The Master will give strength to His people; **The Master will bless His people with peace**.
- Psalm 37:11 — 11 But the humble will inherit the land And will delight themselves in abundant prosperity.
- Isaiah 26:3 — 3 "The steadfast of mind **You will keep in perfect peace, Because he trusts in You.**

Online Version: Peace results from discipleship at work | Digital Business (wordpress.com)

9 WHY WORK?

9.1 IT IS SAID THAT MAN HAS THREE BASIC NEEDS IN LIFE: LOVE, PURPOSE AND SIGNIFICANCE.

Many times, humans try to find purpose and significance in work itself. In Ecclesiastes 2:4-11, Solomon details his search for meaning in a variety of projects and works of all kinds. Even though the work brought some degree of satisfaction in accomplishment, his conclusion was, *"Yet when I surveyed all that my hands had done and what I had toiled to achieve, everything was meaningless, a chasing after the wind; nothing was gained under the sun."*

Other critical biblical principles about work are:

- Work is done not only to help the worker, but others also. *"Let the thief no longer steal, but rather let him labor, doing honest work with his own hands, so that he may have something to share with anyone in need."* Ephesians 4:28
- Work is a gift from God and, for His people, will be blessed.
- God equips His people for their work.

There has been much debate recently about societal responsibilities and obligations toward the unemployed, uninsured, and uneducated in our society. While many of those affected by economic downturns genuinely want to work and cannot find employment, there are a number of U.S. citizens who have become generational welfare recipients, preferring to remain on the government dole. It is interesting to note that the biblical welfare system was a system of work.

- The Bible is harsh in its condemnation of laziness.
- Paul makes the Christian work ethic abundantly clear:
- *"If anyone does not provide for his own, and especially those of his own household, he has denied the faith and is worse than an unbeliever"* (1 Timothy 5:8).

In addition, Paul's instruction to another church about those who preferred not to work was to *"keep away from every brother who is idle and does not live according to the teaching you received from us."* And he goes on to say, *"For even when we were with you, we gave you this rule: 'If a man will not work, he shall not eat.'"* Instead, Paul instructs those who had been idle, *"Such people we command and urge in the Lord Jesus Christ to settle down and earn the bread they eat"* (2 Thessalonians 3:12).

Although God's original design for work was perverted by sin, God will one day restore work without the burdens that sin introduced Until the day when the New Heavens and New Earth are set in place, the Christian attitude toward work should mirror that of Jesus:

"My food, said Jesus, is to do the will of him who sent me and to finish his work."

John 4:34

Work is of no value except when God is in it.

Source: What does the Bible say about work? | GotQuestions.org

Online Version: It is said that man has three basic needs in life: love, purpose and significance. | Digital Business (wordpress.com)

9.2 WHAT DOES THE BIBLE SAY ABOUT WORK?

We spend most of our waking lives working. That is what God wants us to do.

- Why is that?
- Is that the way God really wants it?
- Does the bible have anything to say about the nature of work?
- Did Jesus weigh in on work?

Read the beginning of an essay penned by Bob Black in 1985 entitled "The Abolition of Work" read:

> "**No one should ever work.** Work is the source of all the misery in the world. Almost any evil you would care to name comes from working or from living in a world designed for work. **To stop suffering, we must stop working.**"

In a leisure-loving culture, many would wholeheartedly echo Black's sentiment. Americans spend approximately 50 percent of their waking hours devoted to work. Is work a curse, or is it something that humans were uniquely designed to do? In stark contrast to the assertions of Bob Black, the significance and beneficial nature of work is a resounding theme in the Bible.

The origin of work is depicted in the book of Genesis. In the opening passage, God is the primary worker, busy with the creation of the world.

- The Bible states that God worked for six days and rested on the seventh day.
- These passages reveal that God was the first to do work on the earth.
- Therefore, legitimate work reflects the activity of God.
- Because God is inherently good, work is also inherently good.

> Let the thief no longer steal, **but rather let him labor, doing honest work with his own hands, so that he may have something to share with anyone in need.**[77]

Ephesians 4:28

Genesis 1:31 declares that, when God viewed the fruit of His labor, He called it "very good." God examined and assessed the quality of His work, and when He

---

[77] *The Holy Bible: English Standard Version.* (2016). (Eph 4:28). Wheaton, IL: Crossway Bibles.

decided that He had done an excellent job, He took pleasure in the outcome. By this example, work should be productive. Work should be conducted in a way that produces the highest quality outcome. The reward for work is the honor and satisfaction that comes from a job well done.

God reveals Himself to the world by His work. Through natural revelation, God's existence is made known to every person on earth. Thus, work reveals something about the one doing the work. It exposes underlying character, motivations, skills, abilities, and personality traits.

Jesus echoed this principle when He declared that bad trees produce only bad fruit and good trees only good fruit. Isaiah shows that God created man for His own glory. Paul challenges us that whatever we do should be to His glory. The term *glorify* means "to give an accurate representation." Therefore, work done by Christians should give the world a correct picture of God in righteousness, faithfulness, and excellence.

God created man in His image with characteristics like Him. He created man to work with Him in the world. God planted a garden and put Adam in it to cultivate and keep it. Additionally, Adam and Eve were to subdue and rule over the earth.

- What does this original work mandate mean?
- To cultivate means to foster growth and to improve.
- To keep means to preserve from failure or decline.
- To subdue means to exercise control and discipline.
- Rule over means to administer, take responsibility for, and make decisions.

This mandate applies to all vocations. The 15th-century Reformation leaders saw an occupation as a ministry before God. Jobs should be acknowledged as ministries, and workplaces should be considered as mission fields. The real work in God's kingdom is done in the marketplace and not in "church buildings."

The Fall of Man depicted in Genesis 3 generated a change in work. In response to Adam's sin, God pronounced several judgments, the most severe of which is death. However, labor and the results of labor figure centrally in the rest of the judgments. God cursed the ground. Work became difficult. The word *toil* is used, implying challenge, difficulty, exhaustion, and struggle.

- Work itself was still good, but man must expect that it will be carried out by "the sweat of his brow."
- Also, the result will not always be positive.
- Although man will eat the plants of the field, the field will also produce thorns and thistles.
- Hard work and effort will not always be rewarded in the way the laborer expects or desires.

It is also noted that man would be eating from the produce of the field, not the garden. A garden is symbolic of an earthly paradise made by God as a safe enclosure. Gardens also symbolize purity and innocence. The earth or field, on the other hand, is an unbounded, unprotected space and an emphasis on loss of inhibition and worldliness. Therefore, the work environment can be hostile, especially to followers of Jesus. As we will see, faith at work will lead to persecution.

Some questions to consider:

- What has Jesus asked me to do that I am not doing?
- How can I "take up my cross" daily at work?
- What does it mean to "lose my life" for my co-workers?
- How should I test myself to see if I am faithful at work? Am I getting helpful feedback?
- What is the leadership model we see in the Jesus Manifesto?
- How can I be a happy leader who is favored by God?

Online Version: What does the bible say about work? | Digital Business (wordpress.com)

9.3 IS WORK ORDAINED BY GOD?

Work is ordained by God. God works. God created us in his image. Work is good. We are blessed when we work. It is not about the pay. It is about bringing glory to God who knows what he is doing. Work is ordained by God. If God places us in a position of leadership because we have a servant's heart and place ourselves last, we will show others that work is ordained by God.

> So, God created man in his own image; he created him in the image of God; he created them male and female. 28 God blessed them, and God said to them, "**Be fruitful, multiply, fill the earth, and subdue it. Rule the fish of the sea, the birds of the sky, and every creature that crawls on the earth.**"

Genesis 1:27–28 (CSB)

Good news: God works. God shows us the way. Work, in the Jesus Way, is good and virtuous. Work is the norm. We work most of the time with a day off. That creates a rhythm in our life.

The goal is to work and be productive. Work leads to fulfillment. Fulfillment leads to wisdom. That is a particularly good thing. We control our work. In the Jesus way, work does not control us. We are at peace. After our work is done, we wait to hear "Well done you good and faithful slave."

- Exodus 20:9 (CSB) — 9 **You are to labor six days and do all your work**,
- Psalm 104:23 (CSB) — 23 **Man goes out to his work and to his labor until evening.**

God can do anything: God could have made a world where we do not work. In his sovereignty, which is not what he chose to do. God knows the value of work. God knows it is good for us. God did it for his glory. That is what we need to know and to focus on every day. God gave us this work. Let us be excellent in it.

Consider this: It is important to our faith at work that we live out an attitude that work is good. We should respect those who work hard and produce excellent results.

Some questions to consider:

- Are we excited about our work?
- Do we see our work as an opportunity to express our faith?
- Are we at peace at work?
- Do we see work as God does?

Online Version: Is work ordained by God? | Digital Business (wordpress.com)

9.4 DOES OUR WORK MAKE A DIFFERENCE?

The backdrop to this section is the feeding of the five thousand. It is a stunning miracle. Jesus was moved not to allow the crowd to go hungry. Jesus took care of their physical needs since they could not afford to take them out for a meal. They were extremely impressed.

So, what is Jesus' take on it all.

> Truly, truly, I say to you, you seek Me, not because you saw signs, but because you ate of the loaves and were filled. **Do not work for the food that perishes, but for the food that endures for eternal life, which the Son of Man will give you.** For it is on him that God the Father has set **his seal**.

John 6:26-27

For what am I working? Jesus must set me straight. While Jesus will take care of my physical needs including feeding me, Jesus challenges me to not focus on working for money here. Everything I am working for here is going to perish. It is useless and futile. Jesus wants me to work for what is enduring. That is in the spiritual realm and His Kingdom, not the physical realm.

God's goal for us at work: As we learn how to live our faith out at work, we should get clear on focusing on the spiritual and not the material. It is easy to think of the material, corporate aspects of work. With Jesus, which is not the goal. If our work is to make a difference, it must start in the spiritual realm.

What is the seal of God? There are five verses in the Bible that refer to a "seal of God" or an object or person sealed by God (John 6:27; 2 Timothy 2:19; Revelation 6:9; 7:2; and 9:4). The word *sealed* in the New Testament comes from a Greek word (σφραγίζω sphragizō, sfrag-id´-zo) that means "to stamp with a private mark" in the interest of keeping something secret or protecting or preserving the sealed object. Seals were used for official business: a Roman centurion, for instance, might have sealed a document that was meant only for the eyes of his superior. If the seal were broken, the one receiving the document would know that the letter had been tampered with or read by someone other than the sealer.

Jesus the Messiah bore the seal of God: *"On him God the Father has placed his seal of approval"* (John 6:27). Those who trust in Jesus also have the seal of God, which is the Holy Spirit: *"You also were included in the Messiah [Christ] when you heard the* *message of truth, the good news of your salvation. When you believed, you were marked in him with a seal, the promised Holy Spirit, who is a deposit guaranteeing our inheritance until the redemption of those who are God's possession"* (Ephesians 1:13–14). It is good to know that as a child of God, I am sealed, secure, and sustained amid the wickedness of this transitory world and have the Holy Spirit as the mark of God's seal.

In the Jesus Manifesto, Jesus says several things remarkably similar. *"**Do not store up for yourselves treasures on earth**, where moth and rust destroy, and where thieves break in and steal. But store up for yourselves treasures in heaven, where moth and rust do not destroy, and where thieves do not break in and steal. For where your treasure is, there your heart will be also."* — Matthew 6:19-21 And again, *"You cannot serve both God and Money."* —Matthew 6:24 |

- This is a drum Jesus keeps beating.
- It is not about being wealthy and making a ton of money, here in this world.
- I need to focus on Kingdom wealth in heaven.

To be completely transparent, Jesus continues to elaborate what he means (John 6:28-40)

This is the work of God, that you believe in Him whom He has sent." ... "Truly, truly, I say to you, it is not Moses who has given you the bread out of heaven, but **it is My Father who gives you the true bread out of heaven**. For the bread of God is that which comes down out of heaven and gives life to the world.

Now Jesus gets even more specific.

I am the bread of life; he who comes to Me will not hunger, and he who believes in Me will never thirst. But I said to you that you have seen Me, and yet do not believe. All that the Father gives Me will come to Me, and the one who comes to Me I will certainly not cast out. For **I have come down from heaven, not to do My own will, but the will of Him who sent Me**. This is the will of Him who sent Me, that of all that He has given Me I lose nothing but raise it up on the last day. For this is the will of My Father, that everyone who beholds the Son and believes in Him will have eternal life, and I Myself will raise him up on the last day.

Κύριε Ἰησοῦ Χριστέ, Υἱέ τοῦ Θεοῦ, ἐλέησόν με τὸν ἁμαρτωλόν

Translated: "Master Jesus the Messiah, Son of God, have mercy on me, a sinner"

Online Version: Does our work make a difference? | Digital Business (wordpress.com)

9.5 How solid is our foundation at work?

> "Therefore, everyone who hears these words of Mine, and acts on them, will **be like a wise man who built his house on the rock**. [25] And the rain fell, and the floods came, and the winds blew and slammed against that house; and yet **it did not fall, for it had been founded on the rock.** [26] And everyone who hears these words of Mine, and does not act on them, will be like a foolish man who built his house on the sand. [27] And the rain fell, and the floods came, and the winds blew and slammed against that house; and it fell—and its collapse was great."

~Jesus (Matthew 7:24-29)

Jesus challenges us to be wise in ways at work. We need a solid foundation. We will not find in our corporate training programs. I am guessing you will not find a course at work on "*The Importance of Loving your Colleagues*" Your CEO is not on the faculty.

Here is what a foundation could look like. This is what Jesus teaches us.

- Fortunate [blessed] are the **poor in spirit**, for the kingdom of heaven is theirs.
- Fortunate are those who **mourn**, for they will be comforted.
- Fortunate are the **humble**, for they will inherit the earth.
- Fortunate are those who **hunger and thirst for righteousness**, for they will be filled.
- Fortunate are the **merciful**, for they will be shown mercy.
- Fortunate are the **pure in heart**, for they will see God.
- Fortunate are the **peacemakers**, for they will be called sons of God.
- Fortunate are those who are **persecuted because of righteousness**, for the kingdom of heaven is theirs."

Here is more. It is based on growing in the "fruit of the Spirit."

It is all about growing and maturity. Are we growing in the following areas?

- Love
- Joy
- Peace
- Patience
- Kindness
- Goodness
- Faithfulness
- Gentleness

- Self-Control

This should keep our personal development plans packed with plenty to focus on every day.

> *When Jesus had finished these words, the crowds were amazed at His teaching;* [29] *for He was teaching them as one who had authority, and not as their scribes.* [78]

~Jesus (Matthew 7:24-29)

Online Version: How solid is our foundation at work? | Digital Business (wordpress.com)

---

[78] *New American Standard Bible*. (2020). (Mt 7:24–29). La Habra, CA: The Lockman Foundation.

10 WHAT MAKES A CHRISTIAN COMPANY?

Consider this from Hugh Whelchel. Hugh is Executive Director of the Institute for Faith, Work & Economics and author of <u>How Then Should We Work? Rediscovering the Biblical Doctrine of Work</u>. Hugh has a Master of Arts in Religion and brings over 30 years of diverse business experience to his leadership at IFWE.

> *What we need to be focusing on is not whether we have Christian businesses, but whether we have Christian businessmen who integrate their convictions and principles with their work.*

> *How do we define "Christian" for businesses? Does it mean that the management or ownership is Christian? Does it mean that all the employees sign a statement of faith? Does it mean that you only sell Christian products? Does it mean that your company plays Christian music or puts Bible verses on its packaging?*

> *It is important for Christians to remember why they are in business to begin with. We should concentrate on the most important part of owning and operating a company: making our businesses into good <u>businesses</u>. And the best business is a profitable business. It is profitable because it is effectively serving the needs of others.*

> *Steve Garber, founder of the <u>Washington Institute for Faith, Vocation, and Culture</u>, serves as a consultant for businessmen in several large corporations. He helps them to weave their Christian beliefs with the way they run their companies, <u>asking</u>,*

> *Can we find our way to seeing the health of business as more complex than simply maximizing shareholder profit, to one that in fact addresses profit, people, and planet at the same time — and therefore a more sustainable profitability?*

Garber understands that biblical principles can inform the way we do business, taking our focus away from self-centered, unethical, and short-term tactics for making a profit. If we apply our Christian beliefs to the way we do business, we will focus instead on sustainability, serving others, and long-term profitability.

Living Faith Through Work

Christians in business should strive to live their faith through work. This means:

- Supplying high-quality customer service.
- Being honest and upstanding in every transaction.
- Stewarding one's resources effectively.
- Producing high-quality goods and services.
- Treating every single employee with dignity.
- Looking to serve others and create value.

Of course, these are things that every business owner should be doing. But since Christians live to serve God and uphold the principles set out by the Bible, we should be particularly intentional about running our businesses well.

Titus 3:8 emphasizes that Christ sacrificed himself for us so "that those who have trusted in God may be careful to devote themselves to doing what is good. These things are excellent and profitable for everyone." Since Christ saved us and renewed us, he calls us to turn around and work toward the well-being and renewal of the rest of the world.

Business owners have a unique opportunity to affect society by serving their customers, creating jobs, and contributing to the overall well-being of their communities. They are furthering God's kingdom here on earth.

Christians should look primarily to create companies that cultivate an outstanding reputation, have a corporate culture that exemplifies biblical principles, and create genuine value for their customers. A Christian *business owner could be doing this very well without running a specifically "Christian" business.*

In his book, Redeeming Law, *Michael P. Schutt speaks to this issue as he remembers his own experience as a young Christian lawyer trying to understand how to integrate his faith with his legal practice.*

We wanted to be more than Christians muddling through the law. We wanted to be Christian lawyers; our faith integrated with our calling.

The same applies to the businessman. Rather than asking "Should my company be Christian?" it is more helpful to first ask, "How can I run my business in the most biblical manner? How can I make others ask, 'What's different about this business?'"

Businesses With Beliefs: What Makes a Company Christian? - The Stream

11 WHAT DOES JESUS HAVE TO SAY?

Jesus has a lot to say. Hearing it directly from Jesus makes all the difference. Here is a summary of His teachings. They all have implications for our faith at work.

11.1 MAIN TEACHINGS

1. **Love God above all.** (Matthew 22:37-39)

2. **Love your neighbor [co-workers] as yourself.** (Matthew 22:37-39)

3. **Treat others [co-workers] as you wish to be treated.** (Luke 6:31)

4. **Imitate the Good Samaritan at work.** (Luke 10:37)

11.2 GOD AND JESUS

5. **Change your mind (aka Repent).** (Matthew 4:17)

6. **Believe the Good News.** (Mark 1:15)

7. **Have faith in God.** (Mark 11:22)

8. **Fear God.** (Luke 12:5)

9. **Worship and serve God only.** (Matthew 4:10)

10. **Do not put God to the test.** (Matthew 4:7)

11. **Trust in Jesus as we trust in God.** (John 14:1)

12. **Come to me and drink.** (John 7:37)

13. **Come to me those who are overworked and tired.** (Matthew 11:28)

14. **Take up my yoke and work for me.** (Matthew 11:29)

15. **Come, follow me.** (Matthew 4:19)

16. **Let the dead bury the dead.** (Matthew 8:22)

11.3 OBEY JESUS

17. **Hear, if you have ears to hear.** (Mark 4:23)

18. **Obey my commandments.** (John 14:15, 21, 23)

19. **Strive to enter by the narrow gate.** (Matthew 7:13, Luke 13:24)

20. **Walk while you still have the Light.** (John 12:35-36)

21. **Remain in me.** (John 15:4)

22. **Remain in my love.** (John 15:9)

23. **Cut off anything that causes you to miss God's goal (aka sin).** (Matthew 8:8-9)

24. **Be perfect, as God is perfect.** (Matthew 5:48)

11.4 LOVE, FORGIVE AND JUDGE.

25. **Love each other as I have loved you.** (John 13:34)

26. **Care for the sheep.** (John 21:15-17)

27. **Do not lord it over one another.** (Luke 22:25-26)

28. **Have salt amongst yourselves and peace with one another.** (Mark 9:50)

29. **Do not murmur amongst yourselves.** (John 6:43)

30. **Do not condemn others.** (Luke 6:37)

31. **Judge righteously and not by appearance.** (John 7:24)

32. **Reconcile with your brother before making your offering to God.** (Matthew 5:23-24)

33. **Examine yourself before correcting your brother.** (Matthew 7:5)

34. **If your brother sins, rebuke him.** (Luke 17:3)

35. **If your brother sins against you, talk to him privately and show him his fault.** (Matthew 18:15)

36. **If your brother says, "I repent," forgive him.** (Luke 17:4)

37. **If he who sinned does not listen to you, involve two or three witnesses.** (Matthew 18:16)

38. **If he does not listen to the two or three witnesses, involve the whole church.** (Matthew 18:17)

39. **If he does not listen to the church, treat him as an unbeliever.** (Matthew 18:17)

40. **Be merciful, as God is merciful.** (Luke 6:36)

11.5 PRAYER AND FASTING

41. **Fast in secret.** (Matthew 6:16-18)

42. **Be alert and pray, so that you do not fall into temptation.** (Matthew 26:41)

43. **Pray in secret.** (Matthew 6:5-6)

44. **Do not use vain repetitions when praying.** (Matthew 6:7-8)

45. **When praying, follow the pattern in 'Our Father.'** (Luke 11:2-4, Matthew 6:9-13)

46. **When praying, forgive others.** (Mark 11:25)

47. **Ask God to send workers to the field.** (Matthew 9:38)

48. **Ask, look for, and call.** (Matthew 7:7)

49. **Believe that you will receive when you are asking in prayer.** (Mark 11:24)

11.6 RELIGION

50. **Do not think that I have come to abolish the law or the prophets.** (Matthew 5:17)

51. **Make sure that the light you believe you have is not darkness.** (Luke 11:35)

52. **Be careful how you hear.** (Luke 8:18)

53. **Listen to religious leaders but do not follow their example.** (Matthew 23:2-3)

54. **Keep away from religious leaders and politicians.** (Mark 8:15, Matthew 16:12, Luke 12:1)

55. **Be careful of false prophets.** (Matthew 7:15)

56. **Be careful of the teachers of the law.** (Luke 20:46-47)

57. **Do not use titles of respect for yourselves or others.** (Matthew 23:8-10)

58. **Do not swear in any way, or for any reason.** (Matthew 5:34-36)

59. **Let your 'yes' be 'yes,' and your 'no,' 'no.'** (Matthew 5:37)

60. **Share bread and wine in memory of me.** (Luke 22:19)

11.7 PERSECUTION AND ENEMIES

61. **Deny yourself, carry your cross and follow me.** (Mark 8:34)

62. **Do not fear those who can kill your body.** (Luke 12:4)

63. **Be encouraged during challenging times.** (John 16:33)

64. **Do not be troubled or afraid.** (John 14:27)

65. **Remember that if they hated me, they would also hate you.** (John 15:20, Matthew 10:24-25)

66. **Rejoice and leap for joy when you are persecuted because of me.** (Luke 6:22-23)

67. **Love your enemies; do good to those who hate you.** (Luke 6:27)

68. **Do not resist the person who wrongs you.** (Matthew 5:39)

69. **Turn the other cheek to the one that hurts you.** (Luke 6:29)

70. **Pray for those who persecute you.** (Matthew 5:44)

71. **Do more than you are obliged to do.** (Matthew 5:41)

72. **Agree with your adversary quickly.** (Matthew 5:25)

73. **Do not worry about how to defend yourself against the authorities.** (Luke 12:11-12)

74. **Do not prepare a defense beforehand.** (Luke 21:14-15)

75. **When they persecute you in one city, flee to another.** (Matthew 10:23)

11.8 MONEY AND POSSESSIONS

76. **Do not accumulate treasure on earth, but in heaven.** (Matthew 6:19-20)

77. **Give the poor what you have.** (Luke 11:41)

78. **Sell your possessions and give to the needy.** (Luke 12:33, Luke 18:22)

79. **Forsake all that you own.** (Luke 14:33)

80. **Invite those who cannot return the favor.** (Luke 14:12-13)

81. **Do not do your righteousness to be seen by others.** (Matthew 6:1-2)

82. **When you give to the needy, do it in secret.** (Matthew 6:3-4)

83. **Give it to those who ask.** (Matthew 5:42)

84. **Be generous.** (Luke 6:38)

85. **To those that ask, do not turn away.** (Matthew 5:42)

86. **Do good and lend, without expecting anything in return.** (Luke 6:35)

87. **If someone takes legal action against you, give more than what they ask.** (Matthew 5:40)

88. **If someone takes what is yours, do not try to claim it back.** (Luke 6:30)

89. **Give to Caesar what is his and give to God what belongs to God.** (Matthew 22:21)

90. **Do not turn the house of God into a marketplace.** (John 2:16)

11.9 WORKING FOR GOD AND LIVING BY FAITH

91. **You cannot serve both God and wealth (aka mammon).** (Matthew 6:24)

92. **Do not work for physical food, but spiritual food.** (John 6:27)

93. **What you receive for free, share for free.** (Matthew 10:18)

94. **Do not worry about your life; what you will eat, drink or wear.** (Matthew 6:25-31)

95. **Do not worry about the future.** (Matthew 6:34)

96. **Make the Kingdom of God and His righteousness your top priority.** (Matthew 6:33)

11.10 PREACHING THE TEACHINGS OF JESUS

97. **Preach the good news to everyone.** (Mark 16:15)

98. **Make disciples, baptizing them and teaching them to obey Jesus.** (Matthew 28:19-20)

99. **Preach repentance and forgiveness of sins in Jesus' name.** (Luke 24:47)

91. **What I tell you in secret, speak openly. (Matthew 10:27)**

92. **Open your eyes and see that the harvest is ready, right now. (John 4:35)**

93. **Shine your light by doing good works. (Matthew 5:16)**

94. **Do not impede those who preach in Jesus' name. (Luke 9:49-50)**

95. **Be wise like serpents, but innocent like doves. (Matthew 10:16)**

96. **Do not give what is holy to the dogs; do not cast your pearls before swine. (Matthew 7:6)**

11.11 MARRIAGE AND CHILDREN

97. **He that can remain single should do so. (Matthew 19:12)**

98. **What God has joined in marriage; man should not separate. (Matthew 19:6)**

99. **Let the children come to Jesus, and do not impede them. (Matthew 19:14)**

100. **Do not underestimate little children. (Matthew 18:10)**

11.12 KEEPING WATCH AND THE LAST DAYS

101. **Stay alert and be prepared. (Matthew 24:42-44)**

102. **Be careful that nobody deceives you. (Matthew 24:4-5)**

103.   Do not believe those that say, "Christ is here," or "Christ is there." (Matthew 24:23-26)

104.   When you hear of wars and revolutions do not be afraid. (Luke 21:9)

105.   Flee to the mountains if you see the "abomination of desolation." (Mark 13:14-16)

106.   Pray that your escape does not happen in winter or on the Sabbath day. (Matthew 24:20)

107.   Keep watch and pray, to escape and present yourself worthy in front of Christ. (Luke 21:36)

11.13   HUMILITY AND DISCIPLINE

117.   'Clean' yourself internally, in your spirit. (Matthew 23:26)

118.   Do not rejoice over having spiritual power, but that you have eternal life. (Luke 10:20)

119.   Do not sit in the place of honor but take the lowest seat. (Luke 14:8-10)

120.   When you have done all these things that Jesus has commanded say, "We are useless servants; we have only done what it was our duty to do." (Luke 17:10)

12 FAITH AT WORK CHALLENGES

What is the challenge that Jesus lays out in front of us at work?

> Then Jesus spoke to the crowds and to his disciples: [2] "The scribes and the Pharisees [leaders] are seated in the chair of Moses. [3] Therefore do whatever they tell you and see it. **But do not do what they do, because they do not practice what they teach.** [4] They tie up heavy loads that are hard to carry and put them on people's shoulders, but they themselves are not willing to lift a finger to move them. [5] They do everything to be seen by others: They enlarge their phylacteries and lengthen their tassels. [6] They love the place of honor at banquets, the front seats in the synagogues, [7] greetings in the marketplaces, and to be called 'Rabbi' by people.

Matthew 23:1-7

Some questions to consider:

- Is my focus the kingdom of God at work?

- Do I care about the truth?

- Am I a blind guide to my colleagues?

- Am I obsessed with the "letter of the law"?

- Am I a hypocrite?

- Is my heart in the right place?

What does Woe mean?

The Greek word "ouai" is used in the following three ways:

1) It is used to express a denunciation, i.e., it is used to pronounce someone or something as **blameworthy and evil**.

2) It is used to express a **severe calamity**, a severe distress or affliction.

3) It is used to express **great grief**.

While these meanings overlap, each one has a different focus. And in each case, it is always the context in which "ouai" is used that shows which specific focus is intended.

Matthew 23:13 – **The first "woe" for our faith at work**

> *"Woe to you, scribes, and Pharisees [leaders], hypocrites! You shut the door of the kingdom of heaven in people's faces. For you do not go in, and you do not allow those entering to go in.*

Jesus cares for people. He wants them to know Him and to enter His kingdom (John 3:16–17; 10:10, 17; 2 Peter 3:9). After rebuking the scribes and Pharisees, Jesus lamented over rebellious Jerusalem (Matthew 23:37–39).

His heart is for people to find life in Him. It makes sense, then, that He would have harsh words for those who prevented people from finding salvation. The teachers of the Law and Pharisees were not truly looking for after God, though they acted as if they were. Their religion was empty, and it was preventing others from following the Messiah.

Matthew 23:15 – **The second "woe" for our faith at work**

> *"Woe to you, scribes, and Pharisees [leaders], hypocrites! You travel over land and sea to make one convert, and when he becomes one, you make him twice as fit for hell as you are!*

In the second woe, Jesus condemns the scribes and Pharisees for making strenuous efforts to win converts and then leading those converts to be "twice as much" children of hell as the scribes and Pharisees were (Matthew 13:15). In other words, they were more intent on spreading their religion than on keeping the truth.

Matthew 23:16-22 – **The third "woe" for our faith at work**

> *[16] "Woe to you, blind guides [leaders], who say, 'Whoever takes an oath by the temple, it means nothing. But whoever takes an oath by the gold of the temple is bound by his oath.' [17] Blind fools! For which is greater, the gold or the temple that sanctified the gold? [18] Also, 'Whoever takes an oath by the altar, it means nothing; but whoever takes an oath by the gift that is on it is bound by his oath.' [19] Blind people! For which is greater, the gift or the altar that sanctifies the gift? [20] Therefore, the one who takes an oath by the altar takes an oath by it and by everything on it. [21] The one who takes an oath by the temple takes an oath by it and by him who dwells in it. [22] And the one who takes an oath by heaven takes an oath by God's throne and by him who sits on it.*

The third woe Jesus pronounces against the scribes and Pharisees calls the religious leaders "blind guides" and "blind fools" (Matthew 23:16–17). Specifically, Jesus points out, they nit-picked about which oaths were binding and which were not, ignoring the sacred nature of all oaths and significance of the temple and God's holiness (verses 15–22).

Matthew 23:23-24 – **The fourth "woe" for our faith at work**

> *"Woe to you, scribes, and Pharisees [leaders], hypocrites! You pay a tenth of mint, dill, and cumin, and yet you have neglected the more important matters of the law—justice, mercy, and faithfulness. These things should have been done without neglecting the others. 24 Blind guides! You strain out a gnat but gulp down a camel!*

The fourth woe calls out the scribes and Pharisees for their practice of diligently paying the tithe while neglecting to care for people. While they were counting their mint leaves to make sure they gave one tenth to the temple, they "neglected the more important matters of the law—justice, mercy and faithfulness" (Matthew 23:23). Once again, they focused on the letter of the Law and obeyed it with pride, but they missed the weightier things of God. Their religion was external; their hearts were not transformed.

Matthew 23:25-26 – **The fifth "woe" for our faith at work**

> *"Woe to you, scribes, and Pharisees [leaders], hypocrites! You clean the outside of the cup and dish, but inside they are full of greed and self-indulgence. 26 Blind Pharisee! First clean the inside of the cup, so that the outside of it may also become clean.*

Jesus elaborates on their hypocrisy in the fifth woe. He tells the religious leaders they appear clean on the outside, but they have neglected the inside. They perform religious acts but do not have God-honoring hearts. It does no good, Jesus says, to clean up the outside when the inside is "full of greed and self-indulgence" (Matthew 23:25). The Pharisees and scribes are blind and do not recognize that, when the inside is changed, the outside, too, will be transformed.

Matthew 23:27-28 – **The sixth "woe" for our faith at work**

> *"Woe to you, [leaders] scribes and Pharisees, hypocrites! You are like whitewashed tombs, which appear beautiful on the outside, but inside are full of the bones of the dead and every kind of impurity. 28 In the same way, on the outside you seem righteous to people, but inside you are full of hypocrisy and lawlessness.*

In the sixth woe, Jesus claims the scribes and Pharisees are "like whitewashed tombs, which look beautiful on the outside but on the inside are full of the bones of the dead and everything unclean" (Matthew 23:27). The deadness inside of tombs is likened to the "hypocrisy and wickedness" inside the religious leaders (verse 28). Once again, they obey God, but their hearts are far from Him (see Matthew 15:7–9 and Isaiah 29:13).

Matthew 23:29-32 – **The seventh "woe" for our faith at work**

> *"Woe to you, [leaders] scribes and Pharisees, hypocrites! You build the tombs of the prophets and decorate the graves of the righteous, 30 and you say, 'If we had lived in the days of our*

> *ancestors, we wouldn't have taken part with them in shedding the prophets' blood.' ^{31} So you testify against yourselves that you are descendants of those who murdered the prophets. ^{32} Fill up, then, the measure of your ancestors' sins!*

Jesus concludes His seven-fold rebuke by telling the religious leaders that they are just like their fathers, who persecuted the prophets of old. In building monuments to the prophets, they testify against themselves, openly admitting that it was their ancestors who killed the prophets (Matthew 23:29–31). Although they arrogantly claim that they would not have done so, they are the ones who will soon plot the murder of the Son of God Himself (Matthew 26:4).

Matthew 23:33-39 – **The closing** –

> *"Snakes! [leaders] Brood of vipers! How can you escape being condemned to hell? ^{34} This is why I am sending you prophets, sages, and scribes. Some of them you will kill and crucify, and some of them you will flog in your synagogues and pursue from town to town. ^{35} So all the righteous blood shed on the earth will be charged to you, from the blood of righteous Abel to the blood of Zechariah, son of Berechiah, whom you murdered between the sanctuary and the altar. ^{36} Truly I tell you; all these things will come on this generation.*

"Jerusalem, Jerusalem, who kills the prophets and stones those who are sent to her. How often I wanted to gather your children together, as a hen gathers her chicks under her wings, but you were not willing! ^{38} See, **your house is left to you desolate.** ^{39} For I tell you, you will not see me again until you say,' **Blessed is he who comes in the name of the Lord**'!"

Jesus' words are harsh because there was so much at stake for our faith at work. Those who followed the Pharisees and scribes were being kept from following God. So much of the teaching in Jesus' day was in direct contradiction of God's Word (see Matthew 15:6). The religious leaders made a mockery out of following God.

- They did not utterly understand God's ways, and they led others away from God.
- Jesus' desire was that people would come to know God and be reconciled with Him.
- In Matthew 11:28–30 Jesus said, "Come to me, all you who are weary and burdened, and I will give you rest. Take my yoke upon you and learn from me, for I am gentle and humble in heart, and you will find rest for your souls. For my yoke is easy and my burden is light."
- Unlike the burdens the scribes and Pharisees laid on the people in a human effort to gain reconciliation with God, Jesus gives true rest. The religious leaders spread lies covered in a veneer of godliness (John 8:44); Jesus spoke harshly against them because He came to bring life (John 10:10).

This says a lot. It is from Paul.

> So I, the prisoner for the Master, appeal to you to <u>live a life worthy of the calling to which you have been called</u> that is, to live a life that exhibits <u>godly character</u>, <u>moral courage</u>, <u>personal integrity</u>, and <u>mature behavior</u> — a life that expresses gratitude to God for your salvation, **with all humility forsaking self-righteousness, and meekness maintaining self-control**, with patience, bearing with one another in unselfish love.

Ephesians 4:1-2 (Amplified Bible)

> "**<u>So, because you are lukewarm, and neither hot nor cold, I will spit you out of My mouth.</u>**"

Revelation 3:16

Uh oh! Here it comes! I better listen up and change my mind (aka repent). I better act differently. I better give up acting religious. I better get serious about following Him. I better give up my selfish self-pitying. I better listen up!

I better get on fire for Jesus and His Way.

People of faith know the Power of God at work!

> "Woe to you, Chorazin! Woe to you, Bethsaida**! For if the miracles had occurred in Tyre and Sidon which occurred in you, they would have changed their minds (aka repented)** long ago in sackcloth and ashes."

Matthew 11:21

- Am I missing the miracles of God?
- Have I changed my mind about who is in charge?
- Am I ready to love?

People of faith are not obstacles to others at work!

> "Woe to the world **because of its obstacles**! For it is inevitable that obstacles come; but woe to that man through whom the obstacle comes!"

Matthew 18:7

- Have I become an obstacle to others to follow Jesus?

People of faith are loyal to Jesus and others!

> *"The Son of Man is to go, just as it is written of Him; but **woe to that man by whom the Son of Man is betrayed**! It would have been good for that man if he had not been born."*

Matthew 26:24

- Am I loyal to Jesus?
- Am I loyal to the followers of Jesus?

People of faith understand the challenge of wealth!

> *"But **woe to you who are rich**, for you are receiving your comfort in full."*

Luke 6:24

- I work hard. What is wrong with the four cars I own? Why shouldn't we get that vacation home?

People of faith always hunger after God.

> ***"Woe to you who are well-fed now, for you shall be hungry."***

Luke 6:25

- Why shouldn't we go out to dinner again?
- It was silly when my dad talked about the starving kids in China.

People of faith empathize and cry with others!

> ***"Woe to you who laugh now, for you shall mourn and weep."***

Luke 6:25

- What is wrong with having a little fun?
- My entertainment budget is reasonable. It is not that much money.
- I do not have a lot of time to spend with the emotionally needy.

People of faith shun flattery and are grounded in self-awareness!

> *"**Woe to you when all men speak well of you**, for their fathers used to treat the false prophets in the same way."*

Luke 6:26

- I appreciate the praise I get at work.
- I work hard and it is nice to be recognized.

Is there good news? Yes, Jesus has given me the power of God's Holy Spirit. I have the fruit of the Spirit growing in me. I can be free of hypocrisy. I declare that Jesus is my Master and the anointed Messiah (King). Jesus died for me missing God's goals (aka sinning). Jesus has been raised from the dead in an incorruptible body. Jesus has ascended to heaven and now sits at the right hand of God almighty.

Amen and Amen! Glory be to God.

Ephesians 4:1-2 (Amplified Bible)

> So I, the prisoner for the Master, appeal to you to *live a life worthy of the calling to which you have been called* that is, to live a life that exhibits *godly character, moral courage, personal integrity,* and *mature behavior* — a life that expresses gratitude to God for your salvation, **with all humility forsaking self-righteousness, and meekness maintaining self-control,** with patience, bearing with one another in unselfish love.

Online version: Faith at Work Challenges | Digital Business (wordpress.com)

12.1 God's purposes in ordaining work

12.1.1 Should people be self-supporting through their work?

Why it matters: God wants us to work. God works. We are made in the image of God. Work is good. Work matters. Our faith at work matters and makes a difference in the Kingdom of God. Sustaining ourselves through work is the way of God.

God's goal: The goal is to be self-sustaining through our work. We may have to sweat to get it done. This is our life. This is the way God wants it to be. We must clearly prove that at our place of work. Others must know we are working hard for God.

The broad view:

- Genesis 3:19 (CSB) — 19 **You will eat bread by the sweat of your brow until you return to the ground**, since you were taken from it. For you are dust, and you will return to dust."
- Psalm 128:2 (CSB) — 2 **You will surely eat that for which your hands have worked. You will be happy, and it will go well for you**.
- Thessalonians 4:12 (CSB) — 12 **so that you may behave properly in the presence of outsiders and not be dependent on anyone**.

Good news: God ordains that we work. God gives us the power of the Holy Spirit to help make it happen. We are not in it alone. God promises that when we work, we *"will be happy and it will go well for us."*

God can do anything: God will show us what to focus on at work. God will give us wisdom and insight. Our faith will make a difference because we serve a mighty God who is in charge. God's will is going to be done.

Online Version: Should people be self-supporting through their work? | Digital Business (wordpress.com)

12.1.2   Should we find self-fulfillment in our work?

The way I see it: Work is an exceptionally good thing. There is boundless joy in work (most days). Work makes for stunning days. I cannot imagine not working. I do not see myself retiring.

Why it matters: God has ordained work for our good and for our benefit. Work is a reward, in and of itself. The lazy have no reward. Desperation is their destination.

God's goal: The goal is to show our faith at work. Others should see our joy at working. There is nothing better for us than work. The work is the reward.

- Ecclesiastes 2:24 (CSB) — 24 **There is nothing better for a person** than to eat, drink, and **enjoy his work**. I have seen that even this is from God's hand,
- Proverbs 14:23 (CSB) — 23 **There is profit in all demanding work**, but endless talk leads only to poverty.
- Ecclesiastes 3:22 (CSB) — 22 **I have seen that there is nothing better than for a person to enjoy his activities because that is his reward.** For who can enable him to see what will happen after he dies?
- Ecclesiastes 5:19 (CSB) — 19 Furthermore, **everyone to whom God has given riches and wealth, he has also allowed him to enjoy them, take his reward, and rejoice in his labor. This is a gift of God**,

Good news: There is no lack of work. There is always more to be done. When we have joy with the work God has given us to do, we are fulfilled.

God is God: God could have organized a world where there is no work. God is God. This is the way God wants it to be. That brings us great comfort.

Online Version: Should we find self-fulfillment in our work? | Digital Business (wordpress.com)

12.1.3 Are we going to be a burden to others if we do not work?

> *Let the thief no longer steal.* ***Instead, he is to do honest work with his own hands, so that he has something to share with anyone in need.***

Ephesians 4:28 (CSB)

God's goal: The goal is to work. To not work is to be a burden to others That is not the way of God or His Son Jesus. By working, we have resources to help others at work.

Why it matters: We are to be servants. That is the focus Jesus given us for our colleagues. Because we love Jesus, we want to be obedient. This is not an obligation that we have no joy in. It delights us to serve others. If it does not bring us joy, we better figure out why.

God is good: God love us. We must love others by working. The goodness of God is to be reflected in our care for others at work. God has been good to give us the power of the Holy Spirit. God grows the fruit of love in our lives at work. That is some exceptionally good news.

- Proverbs 31:15 (CSB) — 15 **She rises while it is still night and supplies food** for her household and portions for her female servants.
- 1 Thessalonians 2:9 (CSB) — 9 For you remember our labor and hardship, brothers, and sisters. **Working night and day so that we would not burden any of you, we preached God's good news to you**.
- 1 Timothy 5:8 (CSB) — 8 **But if anyone does not support his own family, especially for his own household, he has denied the faith and is worse than an unbeliever.**

Online Version: Edit Post "Are we going to be a burden to others if we do not work?" ‹ Digital Business — WordPress

12.1.4   Does our work glorify God?

Consider this: This is important. We all need to get it deep in our hearts and soul. Our work is designed to bring glory to God. It is not to earn money. It is not to help others. It should be strictly to bring glory to God.

- Is that our focus?
- Do we get it?
- If not, what are we going to do about it?

What is the glory of God? Many books have been written about the glory of God. In its simplest form, it is all about God and nothing to do with us. It is God's brilliance and beauty. It is from the Greek word δόξα doxa — Meaning: glory, honor, renown; an especially divine quality, the unspoken manifestation of God. It speaks of the splendor, stunning, beauty, brilliance, and amazing character of God. A simple Translation is **stunning brilliance and beauty.**

God's goal: The goal is to bring glory to God. Do our colleagues see that in us? Is everything we are doing about God and His will? May we focus on God and His glory at work.

- Colossians 3:17 (CSB) — 17 And whatever you do, in word or in deed, **do everything in the name of the Lord Jesus, giving thanks to God the Father through him.**
- 1 Corinthians 10:31 (CSB) — 31 So, whether you eat or drink, or **whatever you do, do everything for the glory of God.**
- Ephesians 6:5–8 (CSB) — 5 Slaves, obey your human masters with fear and trembling, in the sincerity of your heart, as you would Christ. **6 Do not work only while being watched, as people-pleasers, but as slaves of Christ, do God's will from your heart.** 7 Serve with a good attitude, as to the Master and not to people, 8 knowing that whatever good each one does, slave or free, he will receive this back from the Master.

Online Version:

13 WHAT ARE THE CONSEQUENCES OF VIEWING WORK AS GOD'S ORDINANCE?

13.1 WORK IS A MORAL DUTY

> *To seek to lead a quiet life, to mind your own business, and **to work with your own hands**, as we commanded you,*

1 Thessalonians 4:11 (CSB)

<u>Some questions to consider:</u>

- Have we devoted ourselves to being good at work?
- Are we working hard for Jesus?
- Are we giving our work 100% of our effort?
- Are we doing work ourselves or just paying others to do work for us?
- Have we become a burden to others by not working?
- Are we taking food stamps but refuse to work?
- Do we go about our work quietly and just focus on the work?

Why it matters: God has ordained work. God created it for us. God is serious about our taking joy in our work. We bring glory to God when we work. We show great wisdom when we work.

God's goal: The goal is to work and work hard. We should delight on Mondays and look forward to going to work. Dread will drag down our testimony. Others will know if we are faking it.

- Titus 3:14 (CSB) — 14 Let our people learn to **devote themselves to good works for pressing needs, so that they will not be unfruitful.**
- Proverbs 6:6 (CSB) — 6 **Go to the ant, you slacker! Observe its ways and become wise.**
- Ecclesiastes 9:10 (CSB) — 10 **Whatever your hands find to do, do with all your strength, because there is no work, planning, knowledge, or wisdom in Sheol** where you are going.
- 1 Thessalonians 4:11 (CSB) — 11 to seek to lead a quiet life, to mind your own business, and **to work with your own hands**, as we commanded you,

- Thessalonians 3:7–12 (CSB) — 7 For you yourselves know how you should imitate us: We were not idle among you; 8 we did not eat anyone's food free of charge; instead, **we labored and toiled, working night and day, so that we would not be a burden to any of you**. 9 It is not that we do not have the right to support, but we did it to make ourselves an example to you so that you would imitate us. 10 In fact, when we were with you, this is what we commanded you**: "If anyone isn't willing to work, he should not eat."** 11 For we hear that there are some among you who are idle. They are not busy but busybodies. 12 Now we command and exhort such people by the Master Jesus the Messiah to **work quietly and support themselves**.

Online version: Work is a moral duty | Digital Business (wordpress.com)

13.2 CAN ANY LEGITIMATE WORK BE SEEN AS GOD'S CALLING?

> ***Let each one live his life in the situation the Master assigned when God called him.*** *This is what I command in all the churches.*

1 Corinthians 7:17 (CSB)

Why it matters: We hold certain jobs in higher esteem than others. We think everyone must have a college education. That is not God's way. I repeat, that is not God's way at all.

The way I see it: There is honor in all types of work. What is important is to focus on what kind of work brings glory to God. It could be cleaning out septic tanks or being a neurosurgeon. Both are important, both must be done, and both can bring glory to God and His holy name.

God is God: God is infinite, never changes, has no needs, all powerful, all-knowing, always everywhere, full of perfect, unchanging wisdom, faithful, good, just, wrathful, merciful, gracious, loving, holy, glorious, infinitely beautiful, great, and more. God is God. God has designed work for us. We must do it for God and for God alone.

Good news: God has given us work to do. Every kind of job is important. Our work is seen as good, and it will bring glory to God.

- Genesis 2:15 (CSB) — 15 The LORD **God took the man and placed him in the garden of Eden to work it and watch over it.**
- Exodus 31:1–6 (CSB) — 1 The LORD also spoke to Moses: 2 "Look, I have appointed by name Bezalel son of Uri, son of Hur, of the tribe of Judah. 3 **I have filled him with God's Spirit, with wisdom, understanding, and ability in every craft 4 to design artistic works in gold, silver, and bronze, 5 to cut gemstones for mounting, and to carve wood for work in every craft.** 6 I have also selected Oholiab son of Ahisamach, of the tribe of Dan, to be with him. I have put wisdom in the heart of every skilled artisan to make all that I have commanded you:
- Exodus 35:30–35 (CSB) — 30 Moses then said to the Israelites: "Look, the LORD has appointed by name Bezalel son of Uri, son of Hur, of the tribe of Judah. 31 **He has filled him with God's Spirit, with wisdom, understanding, and ability in every kind of craft 32 to design artistic works in gold, silver, and bronze, 33 to cut gemstones for mounting, and to carve wood for work in every kind of artistic craft**. 34 He has also given both him and Oholiab son of Ahisamach, of the tribe of Dan, the ability to teach others. 35 He has filled them with skill to do all the work of a gem cutter; a designer; an embroiderer in blue, purple, and scarlet yarn and fine linen; and a weaver. They can do every kind of craft and design artistic designs.

- Psalm 78:70–71 (CSB) — 70 **He chose David his servant and took him from the sheep pens; 71 he brought him from tending ewes to be shepherd over his people Jacob**— over Israel, his inheritance.
- Matthew 13:55 (CSB) — 55 **Is not this the carpenter's son?** Isn't his mother called Mary, and his brothers James, Joseph, Simon, and Judas?
- Romans 13:6 (CSB) — 6 **And for this reason you pay taxes, since the authorities are God's servants, continually attending to these tasks**.
- 1 Corinthians 7:17 (CSB) — 17 **Let each one live his life in the situation the Lord assigned when God called him.** This is what I command in all the churches.
- 1 Corinthians 7:20–24 (CSB) — 20 Let each of you stay when he was called. 21 Were you called while a slave? Do not let it concern you. But if you can become free, take the opportunity. 22 For **he who is called by the Lord as a slave is the Lord's freedman.** Likewise, he who is called as a free man is Christ's slave. 23 You were bought at a price; do not become slaves of people. 24 Brothers and sisters, each person is to remain with God when he was called.

Online Version: Can any legitimate work be seen as God's calling? | Digital Business (wordpress.com)

13.3 WORK IS SEEN AS A STEWARDSHIP FROM GOD HIMSELF

> *Do not work only while being watched, as people-pleasers, but as slaves of the Messiah, do God's will from your heart. 7 Serve with a good attitude, as to the Master and not to people, 8 knowing that whatever good each one does, slave or free, he will receive this back from the Master.*

Ephesians 6:5–8 (CSB)

Why it matters: God has designed our life to be a life of work. That is what God wants us focus on. We are not to be people pleasers but are here to bring glory to God.

God's goal: The goal is to work as if we are working for God. Our work is to a work of service for our Master Jesus. We must have a great attitude because we are not serving our co-workers, we are serving Jesus.

- How is my attitude at work?
- Am I happy and joyful about the work I must do?
- Am I a complainer who constantly moans and groans?

The broad view: Who does not want to hear to words of Jesus saying, "Well Done!" I want to hear that. I am guessing you do as well.

Good news: God has given us an amazing life of work. It is delightful in every way. Our life is to focus on bringing glory to God through our work. The good news of Jesus must prevail in our workplaces.

- Colossians 3:23–24 (CSB) — 23 **Whatever you do, do it from the heart, as something done for the Master and not for people**, 24 knowing that you will receive the reward of an inheritance from the Lord. You serve the Lord Christ.
- Matthew 25:14–30 (CSB) — 14 "For it is just like a man about to go on a journey. He called his own servants and entrusted his possessions to them. 15 To one he gave five talents, to another two talents, and to another one talent, depending on each one's ability. Then he went on a journey. Immediately 16 the man who had received five talents went, put them to work, and earned five more. 17 In the same way the man with two earned two more. 18 But the man who had received one talent went off, dug a hole in the ground, and hid his master's money. 19 "After a long time the master of those servants came and settled accounts with them. 20 The man who had received five talents approached, presented five more talents, and said, 'Master, you gave me five talents. See, I have earned five more talents.' 21 "His master said to him, **'Well done, good and faithful**

servant! You were faithful over a few things; I will put you in charge of many things.** Share your master's joy.' 22 "The man with two talents also approached. He said, 'Master, you gave me two talents. See, I have earned two more talents.' 23 "His master said to him, **'Well done, good and faithful servant! You were faithful over a few things; I will put you in charge of many things.** Share your master's joy.' 24 "The man who had received one talent also approached and said, 'Master, I know you. You are a harsh man, reaping where you have not sown and gathering where you have not scattered seed. 25 So I was afraid and went off and hid your talent in the ground. See, you have what is yours.' 26 "His master replied to him, **'You evil, lazy servant! If you knew that I reap where I have not sown and gather where I have not scattered, 27 then you should have deposited my money with the bankers, and I would have received my money back with interest when I returned**. 28 "'So take the talent from him and give it to the one who has ten talents. 29 For to everyone who has, more will be given, and he will have more than enough. But from the one who does not have, even what he has will be taken away from him. 30 **And throw this worthless servant into the outer darkness, where there will be weeping and gnashing of teeth**.'

- Ephesians 6:5–8 (CSB) — 5 Slaves, obey your human masters with fear and trembling, in the sincerity of your heart, as you would Christ. **6 Do not work only while being watched, as people-pleasers, but as slaves of the Messiah, do God's will from your heart. 7 Serve with a good attitude, as to the Master and not to people, 8 knowing that whatever good each one does, slave or free, he will receive this back from the Master.**

Online Version: Work is seen as a stewardship from God himself | Digital Business (wordpress.com)

13.4 Can you be a Christian Business?

What is the course of action if you own or are starting your own business? Here is a great article being a Christian business.

Source: Businesses With Beliefs: What Makes a Company Christian? - The Stream

> Some of the largest companies in the United States have been identified as "Christian," and this occasionally makes news headlines. Chick-fil-A, Hobby Lobby, Forever 21 and other companies have sustained scrutiny for being businesses with beliefs.
>
> Some companies have been identified as "Christian" by outside sources because of the convictions of their management. Others have openly branded themselves in this way by identifying with certain causes, printing Bible verses on its products, closing on Sundays, or playing Christian music in stores. This can be a fantastic way to witness if the words of these businesses are consistent with their deeds.
>
> Is there more to being a "Christian" company?
>
> What we need to be focusing on is not whether we have Christian businesses, but whether we have Christian businessmen who integrate their convictions and principles with their work.
>
> How do we define "Christian" for businesses? Does it mean that the management or ownership is Christian? Does it mean that all the employees sign a statement of faith? Does it mean that you only sell Christian products? Does it mean that your company plays Christian music or puts Bible verses on its packaging?
>
> It is important for Christians to remember why they are in business to begin with. We should concentrate on the most important part of owning and operating a company: making our businesses into good businesses. And the best business is a profitable business. It is profitable because it is effectively serving the needs of others.
>
> My friend Steve Garber, founder of the Washington Institute for Faith, Vocation, and Culture, serves as a consultant for businessmen in several large corporations. He helps them to weave their Christian beliefs with the way they run their companies, asking,
>
> Can we find our way to seeing the health of business as more complex than simply maximizing shareholder profit, to one that in fact addresses profit, people, and planet at the same time — and therefore a more sustainable profitability?
>
> Garber understands that biblical principles can inform the way we do business, taking our focus away from self-centered, unethical, and short-term tactics for

making a profit. If we apply our Christian beliefs to the way we do business, we will focus instead on sustainability, serving others, and long-term profitability.

Christians in business should strive to live their faith through work. This means:

- *Supplying high-quality customer service.*

- *Being honest and upstanding in every transaction.*

- *Stewarding one's resources effectively.*

- *Producing high-quality goods and services.*

- *Treating every single employee with dignity.*

- *Looking to serve others and create value.*

Of course, these are things that every business owner should be doing. But since Christians live to serve God and uphold the principles set out by the Bible, we should be particularly intentional about running our businesses well.

Titus 3:8 emphasizes that Christ sacrificed himself for us so "that those who have trusted in God may be careful to devote themselves to doing what is good. These things are excellent and profitable for everyone." Since Christ saved us and renewed us, he calls us to turn around and work toward the well-being and renewal of the rest of the world.

Business owners have a unique opportunity to affect society by serving their customers, creating jobs, and contributing to the overall well-being of their communities. They are furthering God's kingdom here on earth.

Christians should look primarily to create companies that cultivate an outstanding reputation, have a corporate culture that exemplifies biblical principles, and create genuine value for their customers. A Christian business owner could be doing this very well without running a specifically "Christian" business.

In his book, Redeeming Law, Michael P. Schutt speaks to this issue as he remembers his own experience as a young Christian lawyer trying to understand how to integrate his faith with his legal practice.

We wanted to be more than Christians muddling through the law. We wanted to be Christian lawyers; our faith integrated with our calling.

The same applies to the businessman. Rather than asking "Should my company be Christian?" it is more helpful to first ask, "How can I run my business in the most biblical manner? How can I make others ask, 'What's different about this business?'"

Hugh Whelchel is Executive Director of the Institute for Faith, Work & Economics and author of How Then Should We Work? Rediscovering the Biblical Doctrine of

Work. *Hugh has a Master of Arts in Religion and brings over 30 years of diverse business experience to his leadership at IFWE.*

14 WHAT IS THE CORE PROBLEM WITH LEGALISM IN OUR FAITH AT WORK?

One of the biggest risks to our faith at work is one of legalism and the hypocrisy that usually goes with it. Jesus is always clear about it. We must commit ourselves to avoid in the workplace.

> *And Jesus also told this parable to some people who trusted in themselves **that they were righteous and viewed others with contempt**.*

(Luke 18:9)

Some questions to consider:

- Is my focus the kingdom of God?
- Do I care about the truth?
- Am I a blind guide? Do I know where I am going?
- Am I obsessed with the "letter of the law"?
- Am I a hypocrite?
- Is my heart in the right place?

The word "legalism" does not occur in the Bible. It is a term we use to describe a doctrinal position emphasizing a system of rules and regulations for achieving both salvation and spiritual growth. Legalists believe in and demand a strict literal adherence to rules and regulations.

> *And Jesus said to them, **"Watch out and beware of the leaven of the Pharisees and Sadducees."***

Matthew 16:6

Doctrinally, it is a position opposed to grace. Those who hold a legalistic position often do not see the real purpose for law, especially the purpose of the Old Testament law of Moses, which is to be our "schoolmaster" or "tutor" to bring us to the Messiah (Galatians 3:24).

Leaders know the purpose of the law!

But the Scripture imprisoned everything under sin's power, so that the promise **might be given based on faith** in Jesus the Messiah to those who believe. Before this faith came, we were confined under the law, imprisoned until the coming faith was revealed. **The law, then, was our guardian until the Messiah**, so that we could be **justified by faith**.

But since that faith has come, we are no longer under a guardian, for through faith you are all sons of God in Messiah Jesus.

Galatians 3:22-26

We must know what it is to be weak in faith and to not judge at work!

"Accept him whose faith is weak, without passing judgment on disputable matters" (Romans 14:1).

Even true believers can be legalistic. We are instructed, rather, to be gracious to one another. Sadly, there are those who feel so strongly about non-essential doctrines that they will run others out of their fellowship, not even allowing the expression of another viewpoint. That, too, is legalism.

Many legalistic believers today make the error of demanding unqualified adherence to their own biblical interpretations and even to their own traditions. For example, there are those who feel that to be spiritual one must simply avoid tobacco, alcoholic beverages, dancing, movies, etc. The truth is that avoiding these things is no guarantee of spirituality.

We should focus on understanding the genuine issues about legalism in our faith at work!

"Since you died with the Messiah to the basic principles of this world, **why**, as though you still belonged to it, **do you submit to its rules**: 'Do not handle! Do not taste! Do not touch!'? These are all destined to perish with use, because they are based on human commands and teachings. **Such regulations indeed have an appearance of wisdom**, with their self-imposed worship, **their false humility,** and their harsh treatment of the body, but they lack any value in restraining sensual indulgence."

Colossians 2:20-23

Legalists may appear to be righteous and spiritual, but legalism does not carry out God's purposes because it is an outward performance instead of an inward change.

We understand grace and truth and its application at work!

"For the law was given through Moses; **grace and truth came through Jesus the Messiah**" (John 1:17)

"Who are you to judge someone else's servant? To his own master he stands or falls. And **he will stand, for the Master is able to make him stand**" (Romans 14:4).

"You, then, why do you judge your brother? Or why do you look down on your brother? For we will all stand before God's judgment seat" (Romans 14:10).

To avoid falling into the trap of legalism, we can start by holding fast to the words of the apostle John, and remembering to be gracious, especially to our brothers and sisters in the Messiah.

We should know not to accept heresy.

"Dear friends, do not believe every spirit, but test the spirits to see whether they are from God, because **many false prophets have gone out into the world**" (1 John 4:1).

A word of caution is necessary here. While we need to be gracious to one another and tolerant of disagreement over disputable matters, we cannot accept heresy. We are exhorted to contend for the faith that was once for all entrusted to the saints (Jude 3). If we remember these guidelines and apply them with love and mercy, we will be safe from both legalism and heresy.

People of faith know legalism at work is contrary to the good news of Jesus!

- Galatians 2:16 (NASB) — **Nevertheless knowing that a man is not justified by the works of the Law but through faith in the Messiah Jesus**, even we have believed in the Messiah Jesus, so that we may be justified by faith in the Messiah and not by the works of the Law; since by the works of the Law no flesh will be justified.
- Matthew 23:13 — "But **woe to you, scribes and Pharisees, hypocrites, because you shut off the kingdom of heaven from people**; for you do not enter in yourselves, nor do you allow those who are entering to go in.
- Matthew 23:15 — "Woe to you, scribes and Pharisees, hypocrites, because **you travel around on sea and land to make one proselyte; and when he becomes one, you make him twice as much a son of hell as yourselves**."
- Romans 3:20–24 —Because **by the works of the Law no flesh will be justified in His sight; for through the Law comes the knowledge of sin**. But now apart from the Law the righteousness of God has been manifested, being witnessed by the Law and the Prophets, even the righteousness of God through faith in Jesus the Messiah for all those who believe; for there is no distinction; for all have sinned and fall short of the glory of God, being justified as a gift by His grace through the redemption which is in the Messiah Jesus;
- Philippians 3:8–9 —More than that, I count all things to be loss in view of the surpassing value of knowing the Messiah Jesus my Master, for whom I have suffered the loss of all things, and count them but rubbish so that I may gain the Messiah, and may be found in Him, **not having a righteousness of my own derived from the Law, but that which is through faith in the Messiah**, the righteousness which comes from God on the basis of faith,

The ugly effects of legalism!

- **Hosea 6:6 — 6 For I delight in loyalty rather than sacrifice**, And in the knowledge of God rather than burnt offerings.
- **Micah 6:7–8** —Does the Master take delight in thousands of rams, In ten thousand rivers of oil? Shall I present my firstborn for my rebellious acts, The fruit of my body for the sin of my soul? **He has told you, O man, what is good; And what does the Master require of you But to do justice, to love kindness, And to walk humbly with your God?**
- **Luke 10:31–32 — 31** "And by chance a priest was going down on that road, and when he saw him, he passed by on the other side. **32** "Likewise a Levite also, when he came to the place and saw him, **passed by on the other side**.

- **John 7:49 — 49** "But this crowd which does not know the Law is accursed."
- **Matthew 16:6 — 6** And Jesus said to them, **"Watch out and beware of the leaven of the Pharisees and Sadducees."**
- **Matthew 16:12 — 12** Then they understood that He did not say to beware of the leaven of bread, but of the teaching of the Pharisees and Sadducees.
- **Galatians 4:10–11 — 10** You see days, months, seasons, and years. **11** I fear for you, that I have labored over you in vain.
- **Galatians 5:2–4 — 2** Behold I, Paul, say to you that if you receive circumcision, the Messiah will be of no benefit to you. **3** And I testify again to every man who receives circumcision, that he is under obligation to keep the whole Law. **4** **You have been severed from the Messiah, you who are seeking to be justified by law; you have fallen from grace.**

Is there good news at work? Yes, Jesus has given me the power of God's Holy Spirit. I have the fruit of the Spirit growing in me. I can be free of hypocrisy. I declare that Jesus is my Master and the anointed Messiah (King). Jesus died for me missing God's goals (aka sinning). Jesus has been raised from the dead in an incorruptible body. Jesus has ascended to heaven and now sits at the right hand of God almighty.

Amen and Amen! Glory be to God.

Online Version: What is the core problem with legalism in our faith at work? | Jesus Quotes and God Thoughts (wordpress.com)

15 SUMMING IT UP!

How should we sum it all up?

Here are five focus areas for consideration that will make a difference for our faith at work.

1. **Love is the main thing about the main thing.** We cannot go wrong if our mission every day is to focus on love. It should be our passion and mission at work.
2. **Humility always wins the day**. Even evil people at work appreciate the value of humility. Ours is true humility based on our understanding of human nature and our own sins and mistakes. We admit them, repent, and seek mercy from Jesus.
3. **Mercy is real and necessary.** Being people of mercy will separate us from others at work. Mercy will show our love.
4. **Purity is important and not to be ignored.** Our actions must always reflect purity and a right standing with God.
5. **Peacemaking changes everything.** We should always, in our humility and mercy, be advocates for peace.

Here is the whole list from Jesus. Jesus is serious that he wants us to show others the Way of Jesus as we work these out at work.

- Fortunate [blessed] are the **poor in spirit**, for the kingdom of heaven is theirs.
- Fortunate are those who **mourn**, for they will be comforted.
- Fortunate are the **humble**, for they will inherit the earth.
- Fortunate are those who **hunger and thirst for righteousness**, for they will be filled.
- Fortunate are the **merciful**, for they will be shown mercy.
- Fortunate are the **pure in heart**, for they will see God.
- Fortunate are the **peacemakers**, for they will be called sons of God.
- Fortunate are those who are **persecuted because of righteousness**, for the kingdom of heaven is theirs."

We need to keep in mind that God is God. When you bundle all the attributes of God in one unified whole, you have God. God is not just one or two things. God is unlike anything or anyone we could ever know or imagine. He is one of a kind, unique and without comparison. Even describing him with mere words truly falls short of capturing who he is – our words simply cannot do justice to describe our holy God.

God is infinite, never changes, has no needs, all powerful, all-knowing, always everywhere, full of perfect, unchanging wisdom, faithful, good, just, wrathful, merciful, gracious, loving, holy, glorious, infinitely beautiful, and great and more. God is God.

Made in the USA
Middletown, DE
14 December 2024